Tossed and Shaped by the Distant Sea: To Live and To Love

To my friend Kathy

love
Grace
January 2010

Grace Hall McEntee

First printing 2009
ISBN: 1-4392-3269-5
ISBN-13: 9781439232699

Visit www.booksurge.com to order additional copies.

Dedication

To my mother

Table of Contents

Introduction   IX

Sifting Sand – poetry   1

Darkness and Winter Rain – nonfiction   3

In Another Man's Shoes – poetry   7

The Dog Attack – short story   9

I'm Alive – poetry   27

Marge and the Light – nonfiction   29

The Dance – nonfiction   31

Tell Me More – poetry   33

Let's Talk about Living – poetry   35

Lady bug – nonfiction   37

Without Him – poetry   39

Letter to Brad – letter   41

The Garden is Running Wild – nonfiction   45

To Know – poetry   47

The White Rooster – fiction   49

Courage — nonfiction   57

Another Storm   61

A Wing on the Beach — poetry   65

Marcy — nonfiction   67

Another planet — nonfiction   69

This morning Seth left home — poetry   75

Fog — fiction   77

Still — poetry   85

Til — fiction   87

Face Down — poetry   99

John — nonfiction   101

Rescue — nonfiction   105

Search — nonfiction   109

Lone — fiction   119

An Encounter — poetry   123

Fox kit — nonfiction   125

Coyote — nonfiction   127

Breathing Holes — nonfiction   129

To Live with the Tick — nonfiction   133

She Talks to Flowers — poetry   139

Communities Overlapping — nonfiction   141

Remembering John and Music at the Church — nonfiction

                                                                   143

Family and Roots — nonfiction   147

The Look — fiction   149

Your Watching Tree — poetry   157

In Sickness and in Health — nonfiction   159

Movie Night — nonfiction   161

Your Choice, Grace — nonfiction   163

Couples — nonfiction   169

The Red Nun — fiction   171

At the Store — nonfiction   205

Pink — fiction   209

Hurricane Gloria vs. Harmony Island — poetry   223

Hurricane Jeanne — nonfiction   225

Acknowledgments   233

Dream

the floor is sand
the walls are stone
cool damp sand
stones from a river
sand that has lain
for a thousand years
stones tossed and
shaped by the distant sea

I rise out of a dream
Circle the bed
And head
Down the hall
Down the stairs
Past the piano
Beyond the kitchen
Around the corner
To the bathroom
Then, in reverse
Back to bed I go
Without stubbing a toe
Or hitting a chair
Or striking a wall
Without counting I know
How many stairs
And where each corner
That will send me
Back to my dream.

Then one day
I step out the door
And tumble and fall
Through space
I hurtle
Past crusts of old bread
Beyond yesterday's fruit
And land
With a thud
I blink
Then stand
Ready to go
Somewhere else
But I do not know
Where
To go
As I do not know
Where
I am.

the floor is sand
the walls are stone
cool damp sand
stones from a river
sand that has lain
for a thousand years
stones tossed and
shaped by the distant sea

Introduction

Tossed and Shaped by the Distant Sea: To Live and To Love is a collection of fifty linked stories and poems about life, love, loss and challenge.

Set on Harmony Island, most stories emerge from the island itself. You will read a personal narrative about the challenge of crossing from mainland to island in a small boat on a stormy winter night. Two stories — one nonfiction, the other fiction — explore the event of an elderly neighbor's wandering away into the woods and the community's response. "Without Him" captures in poetry the rhythms of a CPR rescue. "She Talks to Flowers" is a whimsical poem about a life-altering relationship with plants. Once, my husband and I missed the signals that a storm threatened: "Hurricane Jeanne" tells the story of our struggle in wild seas to save our boat.

Other writings are set elsewhere, for example: "The Look" is a personal narrative set in Paris. "The White Rooster," a short story, takes place in the classroom. The poem "Your Watching Tree" emerges from the memory of my daughter's childhood.

Organized as a continuous thread of ideas and themes, each story or poem is connected to the next by a phrase that links it to what came before. Written over a period of ten years or more, each now sits in close relation to the next, not by time or place, but by idea and subject.

As I was putting the finishing touches on this collection, a friend through writing, wrote the following: "What stays with me, and reverberates, is...that the book is really a love story — of you and Matt, of the island and what grows on it, the community that you two contribute to on a daily basis, and the sea."

Now that he has said it, I realize he is right.

I believe, however, that these writings are about all of us — how we cope with hardship, illness, and loss and how we emerge as different human beings, individuals with broader perspective and deeper insight, individuals in closer touch with the natural world and with each other.

Sit with me now, knee to knee, as I share my stories and poems.

Grace Hall McEntee
March 30, 2009

My mother sifted sand. For me, creating this collection
has been akin to that activity I witnessed as a child.

Sifting Sand

My hand sifts sand
Smooth and hot.
Without warning
After all these years
She floats up
Through grains
As fine as dust.

My mother
Lies face down,
Arms outstretched,
Fingers sifting, smoothing,
As though
To save
Or hide.

For her,
It seems,
I am not there,
For she
Is sifting sand again

I watch and wonder
A child learning
What it means
To sift.

—what it means—

After skiing at Jackson Hole and becoming ill, I wrote "Darkness and Winter Rain," a personal narrative, about stamina and endurance — and about what it means to live on an island.

Darkness and Winter Rain

Our small Subaru still held jeans and jackets, worn ten days before, when we helped our son with the framing of his house. There, too, were our sleeping bags and pads for that night. Since the framing we had skied at Jackson Hole, so into the car we had also crammed two bags of skis, ski boots, travel bags, and a box of wine. Along the way, we picked up some Chinese food, groceries, and plastic bags to protect our luggage from the rain. Our boat is a twenty-three foot shell fisherman's craft. After being away, we were heading back to our island home.

I was tired and sick.

We had skied strong and tough in deep powder at Jackson Hole, but the flu nabbed me on the last day and I'd been horribly ill with chills, fever, and bone ache, sicker than I've ever been in my whole life. I'm sixty-five.

By the time we arrived at the mainland dock, it was 7:30 p.m., pitch black and raining steadily. We leaned our heads and shoulders into the car, our backsides to the weather, heads and arms dry inside, as we moved, tugged, and wrapped each bag in plastic. That done, we dragged the bags down the wet ramp to the floating dock.

Island living requires accommodations, for example, a car and a place to dock the boat on each side of the bay. Matt walked to the slip where the boat bobbed in the water at the marina, while I parked our mainland car across the street.

Our boat's center console with windshield provides a windbreak. Other than that we're out in the open. I wore my long johns, jeans, black ski pants with yellow foul weather pants over them. Two winter jackets, a snug fitting blue one and a large green jacket that belonged to Matt's mother, a woman much larger than I, and my yellow foul weather jacket ensured that I'd be warm and dry on this cold and rainy February night. My head felt snug in a wool hat, a balaclava, and two hoods. Being "out in the open" is an interpretation. We openly faced the challenges of the night weather but wore enough protective layers to allow us to savor the experience. I felt nauseous and vulnerable, but no wind blew to drive the waves into chop and no ice filled the bay. For this we were grateful.

The bay waters were smooth like dimpled glass stretching from mainland to island. Lights along the shoreline glistened through the February rain. Though no moon showed itself to light our way, treetops and slopes of the island became visible in the distance. I coughed deeply.

On this night Matt took the wheel. I stood in the rain, head down, back to the wind. The drone of the engine and the drumming of rain on my raingear lulled me into a place of slow breathing meditation. My cough subsided in this dreamy state, and I was surprised when we arrived at the island dock.

He swung the boat around. I grabbed the lines and brought us close to secure her. "I'll walk home to get the car," I said, "if you want to unload the bags." When we are away for longer than a weather-predictable weekend, we now leave the car at home. One year while we were away, moon tide stormy waters rose over the floorboards of our rusted ten-year-old island Toyota, sitting on the dock. Days later when we started the engine, water shot out of the exhaust pipe — a silly sight from a cartoon life.

"O.K.," he said." I scrambled onto the boat's storage box and stretched one leg up four feet to the pebbled surface, grabbed the huge dock cleat and hiked the other foot up, then reached down to Matt for the bag of Chinese food.

On the island the night was black. Snow left over from two storms still banked the muddy road guiding me along the half mile to my house. But it was hard to tell what was puddle and what was mud, so I slipped into sloppy ruts (Why hadn't I put on my snow boots?). Low hiking boots and the bottom edges of layered pants under foul weather gear absorbed the muck. The bag of Chinese food felt like a lead weight as I slid along the dark road in the island stillness. No deer or fox rustled in the brush, though no doubt my passage disturbed their sleep.

At the north end of the island we have no neighbors in the wintertime, no one to know the car will not start, no one to know the back gate is frozen shut and the front door locked to keep the northeast wind from blasting it open while we're gone.

I left the Chinese food on the ground outside the frozen gate, and abandoning the car that would not start, climbed into the old blue truck and rattled down the road to get Matt. We heaved the remaining bags into the wet truck bed, then drove along the muddy road to home.

With the two of us playing the gate, we forced it open and charged into our cold house. We heat with wood and drain the pipes when we go away for ten days, so they won't freeze. The house was forty degrees.

Oh, I was sick.

Before going back out to drag the wet bags into the house, I slogged in muddy shoes upstairs to turn on our electric blanket. While we never sleep with it on, we use the blanket to heat the bed, especially when its forty degrees in the house and we know that it will still be forty degrees upstairs when we go to bed.

Matt built a fire in the woodstove. I moaned with pleasure as I slipped into dry sweats, then heated and set out our food. I really didn't feel like eating. That flu nausea kept creeping around the edges — I had gone by the fever and the body aches but coughed from a deep place. I made some hot herbal tea and yearned for my own hot soup.

Where do we live?

We live in an inconvenient place. A place where the house is cold when we come home after ten days, where we sometimes have to walk a half mile in the mud and rainy darkness when we've been away and when we're sick — a place where we sometimes have to call on stamina we didn't know we had.

Most rewarding for us is that we live where we can breathe clean air and still feel pleased to have leaped another hurdle and landed in a soft place, a place that is rich with wild experience.

Fully clothed, with my hooded sweatshirt and all, I climbed into my nest of a bed, and slept a healing sleep, the gift from good energy expended *to live in our home at the edge* of an island without a bridge.

—to live in our home at the edge —

Our home on Harmony Island is literally at the edge of an embankment. But I know that living on the edge can mean something very different.

In Another Man's Shoes

I think I could put my feet in another man's shoes
Defy my birth, stand toe to toe with fate,
And abandon my earthly possessions, if I had to choose.

What in a poor man's scuff would I have to lose?
Though I'd risk being scorned by the rich man's estate,
I think I could put my feet in another man's shoes

And live in a hut on a hill, a lowly man whose
Tools are the knife and the ax. I could think and create
And abandon my earthly possessions, if I had to choose.

If the bush of a beard and prune of a face you'd excuse,
I'd sit in the sunshine and carve by the garden gate.
I think I could put my feet in another man's shoes.

Without television, computer, or microwave to use,
My home would be humble. I'd pack all else in a crate
And abandon my earthly possessions, if I had to choose.

The richest of all is he who has found his Muse
And he, who shares his life with a loving mate.
I think I could put my feet *in another man's shoes*
And abandon my earthly possessions, if I had to choose.

— in another man's shoes —

When I was nine years old, my friend was attacked at our local beach. Our parents said she had been attacked by dogs, but after the "attack" my friend was not allowed in my yard. "The Dog Attack" is a fictionalized version of what might have happened.

The Dog Attack

I didn't understand everything our mothers were saying that day so many years ago. Their voices faded and I drifted into that place in a child's mind that fills in details and leaves questions unanswered even as we grow into adulthood.

Recently, I received in the mail an invitation to attend a beach community reunion. I love reunions, love to see how old friends have matured, and how grown-up kids talk about those incidents that shaped us.

That night I sat with two old friends, women who had been little girls with me. Kitty still had that freckled Irish face and turned up nose. Rose's olive skin was smooth, showing only tiny lines around her eyes and around the smile on her mouth. They remarked on my hair, how it was still chocolate brown and so shiny, but, "Hey where are the pigtails, Frenchie?" Kitty asked. And we laughed. We talked about our own children, and we shared stories about growing up at the beach.

At one point Kitty looked off into the distance, then at us and said, "Remember the time that everyone slept out at the Fourth of July bonfire?"

"Not everyone," I said. "My mother would never allow me to sleep anywhere but in my own bed."

"Your mother was strict, all right," Rose said, "and she didn't like men. She wouldn't even let you come to my house through the back path because it went by Old Joe's house. Do you remember how Old Joe used to chase us kids away from the blackberry patch near his back fence? Whatever happened to him, anyway? Is he still alive?"

"I have no idea," I said. "Remember that was a long time ago and he looked pretty old even then. Speaking of old guys, I've been thinking about Sully and his dogs. And Annie. What about Annie? Does anyone know what really happened to her?"

"I don't think Sully's dogs did anything at all," Kitty said, as if the dog attack had happened yesterday. I drifted off and wondered about Sully. He'd be pretty old now, too. Is he still alive? Kitty was still talking. "I think it was something else," she said.

Rose looked at me. "Do you remember the day that you, Annie, and I walked through that path in the woods, the one that went from Cauldron's Store to the beach? Do you remember the naked guy we saw?" Rose said.

"How could I forget?" I said. "We were shocked. I had never seen a naked man before."

Rose was quiet for a minute. She smoothed her hand over her cheek. "No, but I think there was more going on down there than any of us ever imagined."

I veered away from Rose's opening. I could have asked her to say more about what she thought might have been going on at the outer fringes of our neighborhood. Maybe something had happened to her. I'm not sure why I couldn't talk or think about what had been going on along the path and down the beach. It was hard enough to reopen the story of the dog attack.

My mind focused on Annie. I needed to know more about what had happened to her, but far back in a hidden recess of my mind, a tiny light flickered and a new question formed itself. Were Rose's and Annie's stories somehow connected? Or might I be like the gossiping neighbors, building a story upon a faulty notion? Veiling the thought, I reentered the conversation indirectly, leading away from but hoping to circle back to Annie.

"You know," I said. "I always wished I had a boat. I used to watch the guys working on the water and just wished that I could have a boat like theirs or at least take a ride in one."

"A couple of us actually did go for a ride with one of them," Rose said. "Do you remember that shell fisherman that used to work pretty close to the shore, the one who waved to us all the time?" We nodded. "He was a really nice guy. I can't remember who was with me the day he asked if we wanted a ride."

"Not me," I said. Kitty shook her head, too.

"Maybe it was Annie," she said.

"It was! It was!" Rose said. 'I remember being surprised that Annie knew him. He called her by name, and she called him, um, ...Jake, I think."

We flicked from one memory to another, staying now with Annie.

"Do you remember Annie's brother Cal?" Kitty asked.

"Sure, I do,"I said."He had an awful temper. Annie was afraid of him. So was I."

"Did you read in the paper, recently, that he had been arrested for molesting a fifth grade girl at Flaxon Middle School? He was a custodian there," she said.

At the end of the reunion, we slipped on our coats. Kitty untucked the collar of my trench coat that had folded under, causing a lump in my back. Rose struggled with the sleeve of her purple wool jacket. I brought the sleeve around for her. As old friends do, we vowed to get together again, and we left each other in the parking lot sometime around midnight. I drove home alone, thinking about Annie and the dog attack.

In small communities, rumors spread. Stories are told and embellished, and it is hard to know the truth. Years go by and it seems to matter even more later on than it did at the time of an incident, maybe because it is our chance to revise history or learn from it. On that ride home, I decided to track down Sully. Not Annie. I didn't even know her married name, and even after all these years, I didn't want to deal with her mother.

One day I drove down to our old beach neighborhood. Sully's house looked the same as always, white with neat reddish-brown trim. But the stockade fence had been replaced by a low white picket fence. Pink and red roses wound their way up trellises along the perimeter of his yard. A spunky little woman answered the door. "No, Sully hasn't lived here in, oh, let's see, five years, maybe. He's in the Restons Nursing Home, in Pawtuxet. Do you know the one I'm talking about?"

I did and I went to see him.

On the outside, Restons had a cozy look, like the comfortable home of someone who is well to do. But inside, it had an institutional feel. People sat around in groups, in wheelchairs or on couches. Some were dressed in hospital johnnies, others in their own haphazard style. One tiny woman in a wheelchair had a flowered cardigan on the top and flannel pajama bottoms below. They sat. Not saying anything. Together. Alone. The TV was on, more for background noise than for anything else. An aide directed me to Sully, who sat in the same big room, but further back on a couch against the wall. The man she pointed to was looking around as if he were just getting acquainted with new surroundings. His head was shaved close. No more wispy white hair, sticking straight up. He seemed smaller, but he was dressed neatly in a faded denim shirt and limp khaki pants.

I walked over to him. "Sully?" I said. He looked up with a blank expression on his face. "I'm Frenchie. Or that's what the kids in the old neighborhood used to call me." I put out my hand to shake his, but he didn't respond and I knew he didn't remember me. "I was Annie's friend, Frenchie-with-the-pigtails." He perked up and smiled. Old Sully.

"Some friends and I from the old neighborhood were talking about you, Sully, and about Annie. I had to come to see you. At first I thought it was just to tie up some loose threads in my life. Then I realized that I needed to know more about what happens to kids like Annie when they've had a friend — like you."

Slowly, he rubbed his hand over his head and then across his face as though he were clearing cobwebs. Then, he bent over, actually collapsed with his head down on his knees, and he sobbed, shoulders heaving. A dark-skinned aide, kindness written on her smooth face, sidled up to us. A look passed between us, and she glided by. I wondered whether I had made a big mistake. I'd be able to walk back into the vibrant present-day world of tumultuous school and gangly kids, the scents and responsibilities of home and loving entanglements of family. Sully would remain here, alone, with the TV rattling in the background and the continuously running unchangeable film of memories playing in his head.

The aide brought a box of tissues from the table in the middle of the room, and I tucked one into Sully's hand. As a kid, I hadn't even known Sully except to say, Hi Sully, a hundred times or more during my childhood. Now, I put my hand on his shoulder until he calmed down. He straightened himself up on the couch, patted the spot next to him and I sat down.

He looked down at his lap for a minute, cleared his throat, then with the stunning clarity of a well-practiced story teller, he shared the story of Annie and his dogs.

"There's a lot I don't remember these days," he said, wiping his eyes, "but some things I see as clear as the picture on that TV over there. You asked about Annie. O.K., Frenchie-with-the-pigtails," (I saw a glint of the old Sully then) "let me tell you about Annie and my dogs.

"I heard a lot, living next door so close to Annie's house. If I'd had a ten-foot arm I could've tapped at her window. Then she would've pushed aside her ruffled white curtain, smiled and waved. I'd know she was all right. Her window faced my back yard where the dogs played. Annie told me she sat on her bed, right there beside that window, reading the comic books I gave her. She sat there, read and watched my dogs. Red and Redder were her friends.

"Annie knew I looked out for her and she loved the dogs. She had a broken down stool she climbed on so she could pat my dogs over the stockade fence. They'd stand on their hind legs, front paws against the fence, wagging tails and tongues hanging out, waiting for a scratch behind their ears. Annie's mother wouldn't let her come into my yard. Maybe she thought I was dangerous, an old man living alone with his Irish Setters. Or maybe she thought I'd find out too much."

It was almost as though Sully didn't know I was there, sitting beside him at Restons. An old man now, he was clearly revisiting the past, and he continued with his story.

"One day Annie was probably sitting on her bed, hugging her knees the way I'd seen her when she read on the grass in her back yard. I heard a commotion and the mother yelling. 'How could you do that to your sister, Cal! In this house keep your hands off Annie. Look at her arm!'

"I felt my blood pressure rising. I was angry and hot. I'd seen the black and blue on Annie's arm before.

"Cal yelled, 'Don't tell me what to do!' I heard his fist crash into the wall or something.

"When a lamp smashed, I pictured Annie bolting from her bed and slipping out the side door. She ran past my house, legs flying and arms flapping. She was a skinny little girl running like an egret, fleeing from boys who throw stones.

"She raced past old Seymour's house, dark and empty since he died two years ago. She crossed the dirt road toward the beach. I grabbed my cap from the coat rack by the front door, leashed the dogs and ran along behind them to the spot where I could see the whole stretch of beach below. From up there I always felt like Annie's guardian angel. I pretended to be just walking my dogs, but my heart pounded as I watched Annie from the 'usual' place. I didn't want the neighbors talking. They do, you know. Women behind lace curtains, their own histories buried in patched up beach houses."

He looked over at me. "No offense intended," he said. Then he was back into his story.

"Jake, a fisherman friend of mine, worked his long-handled bull rake on the sandy bottom fifty feet from shore. Jake was just a kid when I used to be out there in my own boat. And when I dug for steamers at low tide along the muddy spit north of the sandy beach, he used to talk a blue streak. What's this? He'd hold up a fiddler crab. What's that? A slipper shell. Questions. Questions. But I loved the kid. Sometimes I took him with me when I raked for quahogs close to the shore. For a long time he fished just down below the embankment, near the path that runs to the beach. We always gave each other the wave. Once in a while, I'd slip and slide down the hill and we'd talk.

"Jake's skiff rocked back and forth to the beat of his work, and his big arms worked the rake. Then, hand over hand, he pulled up the rake and watched Annie tumbling down the path. She was so much like the daughter he loved and hardly ever saw. Why didn't men get their daughters when wives were the ones who roamed? It broke my heart. Jake and me. We both knew that. My first wife said I was boring and she left with my little daughter.

"He emptied the shellfish from his rake, and he watched Annie turn off the path and fight her way through the blackberry prickers. I can see her as clear as day, maybe because I've played these stories about her over and over a thousand times. Her shorts caught on the prickers. They tore as she yanked them free. Then she scuffed across smooth clay to the big tree root. There she curled up as if she belonged to the tree, and she licked the blood from scratches on her arm.

"Red and Redder got tangled in the leashes. Red's leash wrapped around one leg. When I stooped to untangle it, as usual, Red licked my face. I stood up, and watched Jake watch Annie. The handle on his rake slid through his hands and into the water until the rake's teeth hit bottom again. He stopped and listened. Annie was crying. I knew it from up on the embankment. I could tell he knew it, too, just by the way he stopped and tilted his head. He worked the mud with the rake. The sun beat down on all of us. It was early August and hot. He pulled up the rake and called out, 'Hey, Annie, do you want to go for a ride?' Annie and Jake were old friends, two hurt souls who found friendship at the edge of the water.

"Annie got up, tucked the torn cuff of her shorts into the edge of her underpants, and ran the rest of the way down the sandy hill as Jake brought his boat up to the shore. She waded through cord grass and mud and lifted her leg into the boat. He grabbed her arm and pulled her in, then pushed off from the shore.

"I walked down the road to pass time. Went as far as Cauldron's Store. I tilted the visor of my cap over my eyes. The sun was lower in the sky and the wind was up."

Sully seemed to move out of the internal film for a minute. He looked at me and said, "You remember the old store? Cauldron's looks different now than when you were kids. It's all boarded up, splattered paint and drawings all over the shutters. That store always had interesting smells for dogs, though." Then he was back inside his story.

"By the time I got back to the top of the hill, it was slack tide and Jake poled his skiff toward shore. With his huge hands under Annie's armpits, he hoisted her up and gently lowered her from the skiff to the grass and clam mud. One of Annie's sneakers sank into the black mud, and she pulled it out with a sucking sound. She turned, waved at Jake and headed toward the big old tree.

"I often saw her curled up there after one of those loud sessions at her house, but it was getting late. I knew if she didn't get home soon, she'd be in trouble. So, I unleashed the dogs.

"They charged down the hill and romped around Annie until she laughed; then they sprang up the path again. Annie detoured around the blackberry patch and scrambled up the path. At the top of the hill, she tripped and fell. The powdery sand stuck to her wet legs. The setters bounced around Annie like two pups. They licked her giggling face and nuzzled her.

"Like thunder, the voice of Annie's mother boomed, 'Leash those dogs, Sully, or I'll call the cops!' She stomped down the road, curlers in her hair, big hips swaying, toward her daughter. She turned to Annie and said, 'What happened ta you?'

"Annie was a mess, what with the scratches, the torn yellow shorts tucked up on one side, and the dust plastered on her hands, her knees and her face. She lowered her head but gave me a peak through the stringy blonde hair hanging over her eyes. I leashed Red and Redder and gave Annie a thumbs-up — our signal that's everything's o.k. She gave me the thumbs-up. It really wasn't o.k. with me, though. I wanted to get out of there fast, away from the woman who treated my friend like a stray cat raiding the compost bin. The dogs took me home.

"Sometimes I wondered how Annie held herself together. I like to think the dogs and I had something to do with that. They were my life — Annie and the dogs. And that was enough.

"One day just as I was finishing my cereal in front of the TV — I watched the morning news with its bombing and screaming — I saw Red and Redder trotting back through the open gate like two lost sheep returning to the fold. I felt panicky. Where had they been? How did they get out? But I knew my dogs. They were like kids, leaping and laughing, sometimes getting carried away, the way dogs do. They were male. When they were younger, I used to stud them out. They'd always been fenced in. By a six-foot stockade. How did they get out?

"Right out in front of my house was Jake coming down the road with Annie. What's this all about? I wondered. I slipped out the back door to latch the gate, and I peeked through the gap between the gate and the fence to watch. Annie's face was puckered, different from her crying face. She looked like she'd had a scare, but with a great bear of a man walking beside you, who could be scared. I knew Annie was safe with Jake.

"Annie's mother bolted from the house. 'What the hell's going on? Where's Sully? It's those dogs, right?'

"She grabbed Annie by the arm. I was back in the house and behind my curtain now looking out. Jake's big arms flapped up and down like a preacher, trying to calm Annie's mother, but she was wild. 'And who are you?' she said, like he'd done something wrong. 'What do you have to do with my daughter?' Annie looked at her mother, pleading with her eyes for her to stop. But she didn't say a word.

"Jake slowed down a little and rocked back and forth like he was in the skiff digging. He tried to explain what he saw happen, but the mother pushed Annie into the house and Jake ducked in through my gate. We huddled for a few minutes inside the back door and he told me what happened. It was hard to listen to Jake tell the story.

"He said, 'Annie squatted, siftin' sand between her fingers, near that big old tree she likes so much. You know the one, Sully. Red and Redder bounded down the hill, jumped at her, and knocked her over. Annie tried to get up and run. The sand's so soft there and you could tell she was scared by the wildness of the dogs. They pulled like a tug of war at her shorts, lost their hold, clamped their teeth for a better grip, and tore the skin on her arm. I could see it all happenin' but was too far away from shore to do anythin'. I started yellin', but it didn't do no good.'

"As he spoke, I drifted away, like in a dream. I could actually hear dog and kid sounds swirling in the sand, Annie screaming, gasping for breath, crying with those hiccupping sounds, and I saw her yanking herself away, the dogs clamping their teeth on her shorts, growling at the back of their throats as they braced their legs and pulled on this version of a rag sock.

"I worried that I'd break down and cry as Jake told the story. But I needed to hear it all, so I hugged myself to keep from falling apart and tried to listen. He said, 'I pulled up to the shore, jumped out of my boat and ran up the beach screamin' at the dogs. The poor kid. Spit ran down her chin and mixed in a juicy mess with the blood on her scratched arms and legs. She stood up. I waved, flapped my arms, yelled. But the dogs kep' on goin'.

" 'One dog wrapped his paws around her leg and humped away. She pulled her leg away from the dogs and fell again. Her hands were all sandy, and she wiped her eyes but I could tell she couldn't see. She clawed at the sand, then curled up like a ball. I picked up stones to throw at the dogs but was afraid to hit Annie. They sniffed at her, me screaming behind them. They poked their noses in the sand under her, then looked at me and ran like wolves up the hill. I don't know if I was any use at all, don't know what they would have done if I wasn't there. I know how you love those dogs, Sully, but it was pretty scary.'

"The dog officer showed up and took Red and Redder away. I should've said I'm sorry to Annie and to her mother, too, but I couldn't get past the gate. I was a prisoner inside the fence of my own yard. A policewoman came to talk to me, and I found out that the dogs must've been excited by Annie's first heat. I had no idea dogs would do that. My dogs. My friend. To me, she was just a little kid. "How did the dogs get out?" I asked, but I knew she couldn't answer my question.

"When Annie's brother Cal was a kid and Annie was a baby, their mother and I were pretty good neighbors. I'd go around to her door and knock, and I'd give her squash from my garden. She baked bread for my wife and me. But the worse Cal got, the more it seemed like I was the enemy.

"I still don't quite understand what happened to us as neighbors. One day when Annie was at school, I knocked and her mother didn't open the door. I could hear her wheezing not three feet away from me on the other side of the door. I said in a loud voice, 'I'll leave the squash on the step,' and I went back home.

"After the trouble with the dogs, I couldn't sleep. I'd lie on my right side, then switch over to my left. My hip ached.

Flat on my back I squeezed my eyes shut, hoping to sleep, but the dogs and Annie played like a movie in my head — the dogs wagged their tails and licked my little friend. Annie giggled. Then Annie cried as the dogs turned into monsters, and I cried, too. The heavy quilt that I've always loved pressed down on my sore big toe until I couldn't stand it any more. One night passed. Two. A week.

"I paced the floor and thought about my father. He'd given up on me when I was a kid. He said, 'You'll never be a fighter.' And in a sense, he was right. Kids fought over the silliest things. Whose turn it was to step up to the plate; who got first picks on a team. First thing you know they'd be rolling in the dust. Adults? They fight over even sillier things, like who will make the best President. Why fight about it? You vote. Somebody gets in. And somebody's out.

"I never took action against anyone even when my first wife left with my little girl. I should have fought for my daughter. It's taken me all these years to know there's a difference between fighting against and fighting for. When I heard the thumps and the screams in Annie's house, sometimes I imagined myself breaking down the door and dragging her brother Cal out of there. I'd come in from behind, grab his shirt and force him out the door. Then what? I couldn't get to the next step. I couldn't even get to the first step.

"I hadn't talked with my wife's brother Jeff for a long time. Did I tell you she was my second wife? When she was rosy-cheeked, pretty and plump, then later when she was pale, sick, and thin as a rail, I'd talk with her brother Jeff if I happened to pick up the phone when he called her. He was a nice guy, but naturally he was more interested in his sister than in me. So even though she and I had been married for a long time, I never really got to know Jeff very well. Brother and sister. They were tight as twins. I hung around the edges, made a little dinner for them while they leaned toward each other and talked softly about who knows what, and I served the merlot. I thought for a long time about whether or not to call him for help. Jeff's a lawyer.

"The two things that I cared most about in this world were on the line. How many times my hands reached for the telephone on the wall beside the refrigerator, then went back into my pocket. I knew the dogs might be destroyed if I didn't act soon.

"What really gave me the courage to call was Annie."

I watched Sully, then, sweeping one hand over his head again and another across his face. It seemed to be his ritual clearing action.

Then he continued.

"I remember this like I'm in a dreamy movie. I had been awake since four or five that morning. When the sun slid up over the trees, the mourning doves always came to the feeder. The soft gray of the first dove picked up the gold from the sun. It cooed in the feeder. Green and purple flashed on the dove's neck. Then another dove hopped in, another and another. Pretty soon they were scrapping. Can there be no peace in the world?

"Jeff's voice startled me. I forgot that I'd actually dialed up my wife's brother and that I was holding the phone. I was embarrassed that it was so early. He must have been in his pajamas, cursing the early morning intruder.

'Jeff?'

'This is Jeff.'

'Sully here. Sorry to catch you so early in the morning.'

'Sully. How are you? What's up? Are you O.K.?'

"My reflection in the window startled me. I was bent over, an old man. I straightened up and stood a little taller, then I reached up to flatten the wisps of white hair that fly straight up even when the wind isn't blowing. I talked to Jeff for a long time, it seemed. Cal was just a kid when Jeff used to visit. By the time my wife had died and Jeff stopped coming around, Cal was twelve.

"'Of course, I remember the little bastard,' he said. 'He hanged the white cat. Remember? My sister cut it down from the tree over behind the woodshed. It was too late for the kitty by then. He was one sick kid, if you ask me.'

"As I talked to Jeff, I saw Annie walk out her door behind my reflection. I disappeared and Annie filled the space. Her blonde hair caught the sun as she kicked a stone along the dirt road. She was dressed in jeans and a green shirt, and even though she looked lean and tiny, for the first time I saw her as a young woman.

"'I'm worried about Annie,' I said. 'I love the kid, Jeff.' I felt almost powerful saying that. Then I remembered that my dogs were in trouble, too. He moaned when I told him about the dog attack.

"'Jeff, the dogs might die if we don't act fast.' I said 'we,' and wondered how that sat with him.

"'How many days has it been, Sully?'

"'A week.'

"I heard his breathing over the phone and I knew it was already too late for my dogs."

Sully's voice broke then, and he stopped talking.

Who could know Sully's story except Sully himself. The neighbors — especially our mothers — and we, Annie's childhood playmates — could only listen, and wonder, and speculate.

From a distance of twenty-five years, I remembered that I knew Annie had gone to the beach alone because I listened to our mothers' voices from my favorite corner near the stairwell. I always needed to know more, so I sat on my dog's fuzzy blue blanket, tucked between the stove and the stairs and hugged my knees. A few steps away and just outside the screen door, our mothers whispered about Annie and the recent dog attack.

"They're male dogs, you know. They'll follow any female in heat, tear her apart, the two of them."

"She's just turned eleven years old."

"I know, but there's something strange about the girl. In some ways she's older. She knows too much, probably from living with two older brothers. How old is Cal, anyway?"

"About twenty-five, isn't he? Old enough to be out of that house."

"What was she doing down the beach alone anyway? Tell me that. Who says it was the dogs that got her?"

"That's what somebody said."

"You don't see anything happening to the dogs, do you?"

"I think they were taken away."

We didn't see Annie for a long time after the dog attack. She was recovering a million miles away. Maybe she has terrible bites and scratches, I thought, as her absence stretched endlessly through August.

As time went on Annie seemed not to be "getting better" but "missing." Kids have a way of knowing when the air is different. My mother avoided my questions about Annie and I learned not to ask any more whether I could go over to her house.

The summer ended. My family lived permanently in the beach community. Most of my friends, including Annie lived in "the city." They faded quickly out of sight in September. I had no idea even where "the city" was. I was nine at the time.

During the next summer, my mother discouraged me from going to Annie's. At first I thought it was because she found out that Annie had stolen money from her mother's pocketbook. But how she would have known that was a mystery to me. Annie never came into my yard, never called me anymore, and I did not know why. Had anyone seen Annie? Did she still live there?

When Sully finished his story, he looked better, as though talking had been cathartic.

"Annie comes to see me every week," he said with a smile, though his eyes were lowered. "She says she has a lot to thank me for."

"What does she look like now?" I asked. I don't know why I asked that question.

"Uh...uh, like you," he said, "but she doesn't have pig-tails." He didn't look up.

I am dark. Annie was blonde.

I pulled my business card — Frances Duchant, School Counselor, 555-088-4432, fdchant@bhsnh.org. All school employees have them now. Sully took it and without so much as a glance at the card, tucked it into his pants pocket. "I'll give it to Annie when she comes in," he said, but he patted the pocket of his shirt.

On my way out of Restons, I reminded the nurse at the desk who I was, told her my relationship to Sully and I gave her my card. "I know that this is a lot to ask," I said, "but when Sully's visitor Annie comes in to see him, would you give her this card? I gave one to Sully, too. On the back of the card I wrote, "Annie, *Please call me.* Frenchie."

She took the card, looked at it, and turned it over. The TV was clattering in the emptiness of the background. Sully sat on the couch, moving his head back and forth as though he were checking out a new place. The others sat in their wheelchairs, their bodies tipped to the side, eyes staring ahead. Some simply slumped over.

With body language that conveyed compassion and a look that was full of nothing and everything, she said, "In the five years Sully's been here, he's had only one other visitor, a man during the first year, and now you."

Please call me —

In our small island community we experience living and dying, with what feels like an uncommon intensity. Our population is older. We know everyone in the winter community. Some years it feels as though everyone is dying. The poem, "I'm Alive," is an affirmation which emerged from my own coping with the loss of island neighbors and friends.

I'm Alive

Josie's dead and Horace, too.
And I'm alive, and Matt, and Jane
And Joel, and Sharon and Dave,
And Marcy, and John, and
Ann and Bob, and Chris and Pat,
Cynthia and Malcolm, and Tom, Billy,
And Lynn, and Brad and Shirley and John
And...the rest of the islanders who
Are in some manner or other
Surviving the winter.
At least they are alive.

But what does it mean to be alive? I ask myself,
Especially when friends and neighbors die
So abruptly in the midst of living.
Does it matter that the Brussels sprouts
Still sit on the weathered stalks in the garden,
That the Jerusalem artichokes go undug?
Does it matter that we're out of rice?
That the winter squash froze in the back room
During the deep freeze of January.

Does it matter that my desk is littered with
Unfinished business,
That the filing piles up in my basket
That dust has settled under the chair near
The woodstove,
That mice leave their traces in the bowls
Under the sink?

Does it matter that I love my husband,
My sons and my daughter and those who cluster
Round them, wives, husbands, children, and
That I love my friends near and far more than
They'll ever know?

I ask, What matters?
And to whom?
And I wonder
How might I change my life
As it becomes more clear
That part of me
Stands squarely in the shadow
Of death
While *part stretches each morning
Into the sunshine*
Of the living world?

—part stretches each morning into the sunshine—

"Marge and the Light" emerged from my weekly visits with a friend, living with terminal illness. I witnessed the decline of Marge's body and the growth of her spirit. Each week when I left her home, I felt buoyant, as her sharing became a life-altering experience for me.

Marge and the Light

For many years, while she clipped willow and bitter-sweet near her deck, Marge saw from her home on the hill the lighthouse. Like her husband Lou and her own breath, the light was a constant in her life. Because she loved that ever-present light, she became an advocate for bringing the stewardship of the lighthouse back to the island where she lived.

As time passed, Marge became steward of another light, which shone brighter as her time on earth grew shorter, she a victim of Lou Gehrig's disease. All of us will leave a legacy, one that is intentional or not. Who we are and what we do lives on in both the products we make and the people we touch. In a public way, Marge created a legacy in her work with the island conservancy.

More privately, she prepared other aspects of her legacy. As long as her breath allowed, she continued to coach both basket making and the decorative weaving of a blanket. Her living room also became the center for assembling family archives. Boxes of photos and stacks of albums grew as Marge grew smaller in her recliner. Nieces came once a week to tap her knowledge of people in old family photos and to listen to Marge's stories of their fathers, mothers, uncles and aunts.

Toward the end of her time on earth, Marge was host to many visitors — relatives and friends, caregivers, a priest, a Buddhist nun, and a monk. I was often a fly on the wall during visits and was privy to a unique exchange that occurred. While visitors paid homage or helped, Marge — in her subtle or sometimes not so subtle way — became their teacher. A teacher by profession and always a woman in charge, Marge evolved into a softer but no less intellectual version of her professional self. She valued every person and shared with each something of herself.

As time passed, I witnessed the growth of Marge's spirit as her body declined. Her eyes became brighter, as though a new light had been kindled within her. During my weekly visits to Marge's house, I bathed her hands and feet in fragrant herbal water, then massaged them to keep the circulation going. All the while, we talked about life and death. What happens in the body? What in the mind and spirit? We asked of ourselves, "How does one live well? How does one die well?" then we tackled the questions one by one, bit by bit. Every now and then I'd come back to the question, "What are you learning?"

To that question Marge Del Papa — an independent but dedicated partner to her loving husband Lou, a poised professional woman in a number of fields, especially those of math education and fiber arts — answered: "If I could get down on my knees and wash my floor, I would enjoy that thoroughly."

One day at the end of her life, she said, *"The only important thing in life is the people who share it with you."*

On that day, as always, driving away from her house, I felt buoyant, filled with light.

—The only important thing in life is the people who share it with you—
On Thursday, as usual, I sat with Marge.

The Dance

He hoists her from her chair, and they stand face to face, her arms around his lower neck, his right hand at the belt around her waist. "Don't make me laugh," he says. His left hand grabs her buttocks.

"All set?"

"Yes."

Using buttocks as handle, he lifts her feet off the ground, she a life-sized rag doll in his arms. As though they are sexy dancing, he leads her a quarter turn to the left.

They rest and breathe together.

Then he lowers her into the wheelchair.

I, the witness, sitting off to the side, have seen *all there is to see about love.*

—all there is to see about love—

The meaning of this poem, a ghazal, written during a poetry class, emerged from its form. A ghazal is a lyric poem with a fixed number of verses and a repeated rhyme, typically on the theme of love. So much of my learning these days comes from attention to living and loving.

Tell Me More

I want to hear your voice and the ocean's roar,
Explore with you, then come back to the inside land.
Before we sleep for the last time, tell me more.

My eyes on you, chin in my hand on the floor,
I listen to childhood pranks — how all of you ran!
I want to hear your laughter and the ocean's roar

And hear of the pain, the stuff of life's stormy lore
From the sea — of you with a son in a ship unmanned.
Before we sleep for the last time, tell me more.

It's not what is said, but the saying, the weaving of nets for
The catching of love midst the shells and debris in the sand.
I want to hear your laughter and the ocean's roar.

Wine flows with words of our day, and you lean to pour
A second glass. I see the old strength of your hand.
Before we sleep for the last time tell me more.

The life from your body floats; like a gull it soars
On a freshening breeze, then drops like a rock back to land.
Tomorrow, I'll hear your laughter in the ocean's roar,
But before you sleep for this last time, *tell me more.*

— tell me more —

I am splashing around in the sea of living and loving, but movement has occurred in my thinking. In the poem, "Let's Talk about Living," I have discovered that a universal "I" exists.

Let's Talk about Living

Let's talk about living.
My mother called me "imp of Satan."
Before that my name was Ruth.
Now it is Grace.

Inside me,
Squeezed into a tiny ball the size of my heart,
Sits all the love and energy of the universe.
Lucky me!

Sometimes the ball pops a hole and
Energy leaks out.
For a split second I panic.

Has my heart burst?
My energy gone to Hell?
Am I really an imp of Satan?

Then I smile again,
For shimmering in you.
I find my energy again.

I am you
And you are me
And the energy is still there.

Like found poetry
Mixed and matched.

—*I am you* —

As I reread this personal narrative, I raise this question for myself: Despite my intention to be compassionate to a ladybug caught in my paint can, was I, in fact, being cruel?

Ladybug

It landed on the edge of the paint can and commanded attention. The outer ridge of the can was dry, but some of the inner edge was sticky and wet where I had skimmed excess paint from my brush. Insects are survivors, so I didn't worry about its survival. Still, I looked closer. Here was a ladybug with fewer spots than others I had recently seen.

As I hesitated in my task of painting the moldings in my bedroom to examine this tiny creature, the ladybug somehow lost its balance and tumbled into the can.

My breath sucked in as though a terrible thing had happened. As though? It had. I watched the life and death struggle, knowing there was little I could do. Would a clumsy human be able to save a ladybug by applying paint thinner to its fragile body? No. Not a chance.

The best I could do was to help it to die. As I coated it thoroughly with paint and pushed it deeper into the bucket, a flashback from thirty-five years ago zapped across my mind. One of my children's hamsters was dying. The bite from its mate had become swollen, no doubt infected, and the little critter lay over on its side, making dying sounds. Laurie and Lee were out playing in a friend's yard. To avoid the trauma of their watching a pet in agony, I decided to play God and end its life.

I scooped it gently from the cage into a shoebox lined with Kleenex. I cringe even now to think of the incident.

Beyond the sand pile, close to the bushes that led into the woods, I dug a hole big enough for the box and the hamster. Life still beat in its little body. Burying it alive was out of the question, so I dumped it out of the shoebox. My intention was to pop it on the head with the shovel, then cover the expired hamster in its earthy grave.

Screwing up my courage (I had never before killed), I poised the shovel for the kill. With an abrupt thrust, my eyes pinched tightly closed, I drove the shovel toward the critter's head. And, of course, missed. My body slumped over, eliminating any possibility of a second try. It simply couldn't be done. I leaned on the shovel and observed the hamster.

The wounded and sick little critter chose its time for departure and without a sound expired, there in the hole.

Not so with the ladybug trapped in paint. For interminable minutes its tiny movements attested to life beneath the thick surface. I tried to forget its struggle by continuing with my painting, and indeed, I did allow the ladybug with fewer dots *to drift away*, carrying with it a tiny bit of myself.

—to drift away—

After we moved to Harmony Island, my husband and I became Emergency Medical Technicians. This poem emerged from one rescue.

Without Him

Together we bolt
In the middle of the night.
And leap
At the clanging call for help.

His face is gray.
His breath is gone.
His heart stopped.

We breathe and breathe
And compress his chest,
Breathe and compress,

Then check:
No breath.
No pulse.

Could we let him go
To swim
The sweet sea?

Breathe
Compress...

Breathe
Compress…

Do you think
He hears
The siren's song?

Breathe
Compress
He breathes!
He breathes!

In the dark of night,
No moon, no stars,
The velvet sea, she
Swells and heaves,
Curls and froths,
Then *falls and sighs*
Without him.

–falls and sighs without him—

What do you do when a friend is ill? Our friend Brad was a literary kind of guy, who liked to hold a book or paper in hand. When he was ill and struggling for his life, I decided to send him a letter as a precursor to a possible visit.

Letter to Brad

September 25

Hi Brad,

I'm sorry to be typing this. It feels less personal, somehow without the scrawl of pen on paper, but I have had the card sitting on the table for days. Because there was too much too much to say, I didn't write it.

Since you entered the hospital, Matt and I have been thinking about you and talking about your will to live. Your courage to face the pain for the gift of life feels extraordinary. We talk with Cathy (Matt talks with brother Dick) to keep posted on your progress. All this is to say you are uppermost in our minds these days. With this note we send our healing energy. (These, of course, are my words. Matt would say it differently).

Life goes on as usual, here on the island. Maybe it is that which is so precious — life as usual. We've been to some meetings in town on the mainland about the parking situation for the islanders. Despite the fact that we've heard for years that the mainlanders feel antipathy for the islanders (and we do get a tiny whiff of that at meetings), it turns out that we really are partners searching for a solution to a common problem, especially as the town grows.

On another note, in my garden recently I found a blue butterfly. I've taken some photos of it and hope to get some help with identification from a worker at the south end. I understand that one of the workers is a butterfly expert. My daughter has several butterfly books in her collection, but none of the butterflies in her books match the one I have seen here in my garden.

And the garden is still going. It has been beautiful this year, but as always in September, the weeds are winning. Matt tilled a bit of it under to keep the weeds from actually taking over the whole thing. We look forward to winter crops, like kale, Brussels sprouts, leeks, sweet potatoes, and Jerusalem artichokes. Tomatoes are still gracing the vines, though, so we're not into winter just yet.

My daily walks are always rich in island discovery. Most recently I have seen both piping plovers and semi-palmated sandpipers. A few days ago on the beach where sandpipers were skittering along, I found seven huge oysters. I'm not an oyster cook, haven't even known what to do with the things, but I looked in a cookbook entitled <u>River Road</u> that Cathy gave to me. There I found Creole Deviled Oysters, which turned out to be as lovely as I knew that oysters had the potential of being. Have you done much with oysters?

Our conversation about oysters led Matt and me to examining the inside of their shells. We noticed the dark spot where the muscle is attached and we wondered why that was black and the rest white. Then we thought about pearls and how the oyster creates from an irritant. This scratching thing — maybe something that could threaten the well being of the oyster — becomes the catalyst for a thing of beauty.

So, as I say, things are going along as usual here. It is, after all, *a lovely life* we islanders share, isn't it?

We hope you are improving one tiny bit at a time. When you feel like having visitors, we'll come to see you, if you'd like. Maybe Cathy will let us know if you want that and when a good visiting time might be.

Love
Grace

—a lovely life—

I write about friends who are living and dying on the island and enjoy the richness of being with each one of them on the journey from here to there. In the garden I find a different kind of peace.

The Garden is Running Wild

The garden is running wild, even as it is caving in, exhausted from valiant production. Grass now grows where onion plants graced even rows. Squash vines entangle Swiss chard, celery, and basil, as they creep across the path to the carrots. Dill, which has set up shop in all parts of the garden (What is that? Friends ask. There's so much of it!) now bends on browned and broken stems from Sunday night's torrential rain. Cauliflower heads pose in the center of grand rosettes of leaves, waiting to be harvested. The green bean patch is bare — as was Matt when he picked beans early one morning, naked, and stung by a bee, indignant that Matt should be so close to the hive before the sun was up.

Today I'll pull the rampant grass from the onion patch and plant buckwheat as a ground cover. I'll harvest cauliflower, broccoli, basil (and make pesto). For the first time skullcap has blossomed. I'll check to see about harvesting, and I'll take the spearmint, peppermint and oregano for drying.

"So much to do," I think, but once I *step into the garden and join the plants,* I let go of thinking and move around the garden, a part of the process myself. A slowing down happens. My breathing and heart rate tune to the plants and we're simply in the garden together.

—step into the garden and join the plants—

Poems come from a secret place, hidden until I intend to write one. Then from a wellspring deep inside meaning emerges.

To Know

We ask a mentor, "What does it mean to know?
He says: "to read, to write, to compute is to know."

Two lovers inside the blanket of night know no morrow.
They teach the sun and the moon what it means to know.

Roots of lavender, thyme, and rue in my garden grow
Down under the old stonewall. How much do they know?

Your anger that kindles like fire in the mist of new snow
Brews melting, like raindrops, that someone who loves you can know.

On fringed wings of cawing crows fly darkness and sorrow
Of the dying, discarded – the dead that all crows know.

The storm winds in winter hurl sleet at our north-facing window.
In the hideaway place of our music we choose not to know.

The pores in my skin, the blood in my veins, my bone marrow
Inform me. They say how you are, where you are, what
we know.

She releases her flesh and her bones to the earth below.
What grows there will know *what no one could possibly know.*

—what no one could possibly know—

"The White Rooster" arises from actual incidents and situations, but this is a work of fiction. The story is "true" only in its expression of human situations, not in the facts.

The White Rooster

Sprawled comfortably on the floor with her fourth graders, Hope leaned on her right elbow, fingered the story pages near her left hand — and waited for her fourth graders. Lynne scooted over by Robin, sitting cross-legged on the floor. Erin untangled her straw-colored hair caught on a button of her sweater. Paulie, self absorbed as always, emerged from his own world and looked at his teacher. By springtime students knew that for any gathering, whether for a story read aloud or for a group meeting, their signal for readiness was to bring their bodies, packed with nine-year-old energy, to a place of stillness and to look at her. Tim provided a model for the rest. He stretched flat on his belly, leaning on elbows, chin on one hand, clear brown eyes riveted to hers.

For a split second, Hope's thoughts flew to her own son Leaf, a fourth grader in a neighborhood school, ten miles away. She breathed deeply and said to herself, "Well, here we go."

She had dared to write the story of "The White Rooster" to elicit response from her class. At first she had convinced herself it was to nurture those children who might need to talk about cruelty. Then she admitted that this was not entirely true. It was for her, too — her need — to peek into her son's domain, to know better her own place in it. She sighed. Her son Leaf, a smiley, huggable kid was retreating from her, his mother, to a place beyond reach. He avoided her touch and no longer told her his secrets, those things that troubled his heart, as if he were erecting a cage, within which to keep himself safe. She ached inside his loneliness and wondered how many other children sitting before her struggled as he did.

"Miss Hope? Miss Hope, we're ready," Erin's voice popped her bubble of thought and again she was with her *students*, twenty fourth-graders, sitting on the floor with her. All had notebooks open to jot, as she read, a word or note that struck them — struck them as meaningful to their lives, as something to wonder about, to question, to talk about. They loved to talk.

Hope sat up and crossed her legs yoga style. "This is a story about a rooster," she said, "and about Phil, a boy about your age." She breathed deeply and read aloud: *"The White Rooster."*

Before his father left him in the field that day, Phil was a happy nine-year- old.

Paulie scribbled in his notebook, his face close to the paper, his body tense.

He had fixed up a room off the garden house and made it into a fort, more than a fort really, a kid home closer to the outdoors. The garden house leaned on its foundation southeast of the main house and down the meadow not too far from the chicken coop. Phil had uncovered and cleared the old grass-covered flagstones. By himself he had found little bushes in the field — a former nursery — dug them up, and planted them along one side of the newly found walkway leading to the fort. In early March, he even insulated the room. And, in an old sinkhole that somebody had used for trash a long time ago, he found an old bed frame with pretty good springs.

Everyone jotted something on paper — except for Tim. I'll bet they all have forts, Hope thought. Tim lay still, within arm's length of Hope.

Phil loved to hear the woofs and squawks of the animals around the yard while he sprawled on his cot, thinking. On weekends Phil's father assigned chores for him to do, so he couldn't play then, but he had plenty of time in the afternoons after school. He was plain old happy in his little spot. He had neighborhood friends at school and animal friends at home.

Harry, the Bantam rooster, was the funniest of the yard animals. He crowed at all the wrong times. Phil laughed just thinking about him. Sometimes after school, when the kids came into his yard to play soccer, Harry hopped up onto the ball and became part of the game.

The students giggled. No one wrote. She hoped they would remember to stand back from the story and respond as it unfolded.

Now there was another pet — a great handsome white rooster that stood head and neck over Harry. Last summer the patched-up coop had served well for the spring chicks Manny at the fruit stand had given them. They had reached the size of adult quail by fall. Then around Halloween, a night critter — probably a mink — had struck. When Phil brought the feed down the next morning, the coop was spattered with blood. Only two chickens remained alive — two roosters: Harry the old Bantam and a young white one.

Hope's students had been writing fiction from experiences in their lives. She had urged them to fictionalize any events. "Make them much more or less than they really were. Use different names and places, different surrounding details," she had said. "The 'real stuff' is simply a launching pad — a place to begin." She always joined students in their writing and they knew, of course, that she had written

"The White Rooster." Would they know Hope was "Mom?" Of course, they would. What a fool she had been. Why hadn't she more carefully fictionalized the events?

There would be no eggs this spring, but at least, for a while, Phil had the two pets — and the roosters had each other. During those winter months following the attack, Harry and the white rooster nestled together in the cold, but in the springtime when plant and animal juices began to run, the two of them fought. A couple of times the white stalked out of the coop in the morning with specks of bright red blood on his snowy breast.

But Phil didn't worry about that. Like the other animals — the three dogs, the pony, the guinea pigs, and the cats — the roosters would adjust, like when Reich the Doberman had first come to them. You'd swear there was going to be a fight between Reich and Kim, the English Setter who was the old master of the yard. That was the fun of having all those animals. At first you'd swear there was going to be a big fight with the new guy on the outs, but eventually the new guy fit in and just flowed with the rhythm of the rest of the gang. It was like that with kids in a new neighborhood, too, Phil thought one day as he lay on his cot.

He remembered his first months in the neighborhood. One time Robby took his hat on the bus and threw it around. Then the kids made fun of him when he cried.

Erin winced. Hope felt a writer's thrill of seeing emotions sweep across student faces. Their bodies shifted. Some jotted notes in their notebooks.

Phil remembered the time Ray and Todd bullied him when he wanted to get in on their ball game. Funny, though, now they were all friends. The white rooster would fit in, too. He was sure of it.

Erin sighed. Her face relaxed into a soft smile.

Of course, Dad wasn't too thrilled with the four-in-the-morning cock-a-doodle-doo's under his bedroom window. Phil couldn't always catch the roosters to put them back into the coop

and away from the house for the night. Theirs was not a farm
family. Farm-like smells or sounds made the wrinkles in Dad's
forehead scrinch and grow deeper, and he threatened to get rid of
the white. Phil would just have to try harder. No sense in
annoying Dad. He had enough to be mad about. Mom said he
was just tired.

Paulie and Robin studied Hope. In their innocence and
caring, she knew her students would want to know more
about "Dad" and "Mom," more than she could tell.

*It was Saturday morning. Phil could hear his mother and
father in the house, his father's angry voice saying something about
work, his father giving the orders, his mother sobbing again, his
mother asking questions and agreeing with whatever answer his
father gave.*

Tim's expression softened. His mouth opened as if he
might speak. But he — and all of them — knew the rule:
Save questions and comments for the end.

*Phil flicked his silky brown hair back with this left hand,
then put the hand under his head as he lay on the cot listening
and thinking, and waiting. In a couple of minutes his father
would shout for him with a list of chores for the day. Flies buzzed
against the dirty window as the sun moved around to that side of
Phil's retreat. The sound mesmerized him and he drifted a little
into a daydream world of kid happiness.*

*"Phil. Phil!" A voice barged into the dream and shot him
up from the cot and onto his feet before he realized that it was his
father's voice — close up, just outside the fort.*

"Catch that white rooster!" his father said.

*Not daring to question his father's order, Phil coaxed the
handsome white over to him. Harry kept getting in the way.
He probably thought that the white was going to get a special
treat. Phil hugged his arms around the warm body of the white*

rooster, nestled his face in its feathers and breathed in, then he brought the white over to his father. He wondered now why they were catching the rooster.

"Follow me," his father said, the frown in his forehead deepening to a scowl as he turned away toward the field behind the house. Harry hung back, sidestepping toward the coop. Phil's father marched out in front. With his head down, Phil followed in silence.

When Phil looked up, he knew that he was in trouble. There standing upright in the field was the shovel he had used yesterday to bury the toad squashed flat in the driveway. He had forgotten to put the shovel away.

Expressions rippled over the faces of the students sitting before Hope. Was it fair that the story offered a moment of relief? Were they remembering a time when they had been in just a tiny bit of trouble? Hope felt a flood of heat. Maybe she could stop right here and say the story is unfinished. Her throat tightened as she tried to go on and tears rose up to the edge of her lids. So much of teaching is learning, she thought. Learning to learn in secret. She couldn't very well lay out the whole fucking marriage for the kids. She couldn't tell anyone. In the midst of family, friends, and neighbors she had never been so alone in her life. Now, like a spy cloaked as teacher, she was setting her students up to unveil information from their minds. To teach her. She planned to use what she learned to work with her son. Hope cleared her throat.

Phil followed, close behind his father, so close that as his father's right hand swung back it almost struck Phil with something black. It was a gun. A gun! A searing flame of fear swept over him and he almost dropped the rooster. Would his father shoot him if he let the rooster go? The question branded him forever while he clutched the warm rooster closer to his own body. The white did not struggle.

Tim's head was on the floor. Was he sleeping? No. His fist was clenched. She continued.

His father stopped near the shovel. He talked to the grass, but Phil knew that the words were meant for him. "When I tell you to let go, let go," his father said as he raised the gun.

Phil's eyes glazed over and he closed into himself. His heart thumped hard and fast, and he felt the rooster's little bird heart beat like a runaway's feet racing for the gate of freedom.

"O.K., let go."

Phil didn't know whether he would throw up or let the rooster go, or both. He closed his eyes allowing his hair to fall over his forehead, and he let go. The shot slammed into his ears and he waited, half expecting to fall over dead.

A collective gasp. Lynne and Robin held hands. Erin twisted her hair. Paulie rocked. Tim tightened.

"Dig the hole," his father ordered, pointing to the shovel.

Phil tried to force himself to straightness, but he reeled and wobbled like a boy made of rubber. He struggled to control his mind and body, so they would take charge and dig the hole for the beautiful white rooster, stained now with bright red blood.

If his father knew what was going on in his mind, his body, and his eyes, he'd surely cuff him off the top of his head — or worse. Phil pushed the shovel into the thick grass, stood on it, wiggled it back and forth until it pierced the ground. He lifted grass with soil attached and set it aside. Again and again, he stabbed the shovel into the ground, drove it deeper, and removed loose soil, then orange clay.

Tears blinded him and his world narrowed to the hole, growing deeper and deeper until he thought he could — and might — crawl into it. With eyes barely slits now in a buzzing head, he stretched his arms to measure the size of the bloody rooster and then leaned down to judge the size of the hole he had dug.

Finally, he flicked back his hair, wet with tears, and looked up for his father's approval. But his father was gone. Just the dead rooster and Phil and the hole were there.

Before she could say anything further, Tim snapped into a sitting position and fastened onto her eyes. "Miss Hope, is Phil your son?"

Hope felt the laser intensity of Tim's eyes. "Yes, Tim, Phil is my son. His real name is Leaf."

Erin piped up, "How did you know what happened in the field?"

"Leaf told me some. I filled in the blanks and made the rest up. This is a fictional story."

Tim said, "Does your son know you wrote this story?"

"No."

He tipped his head a little to one side, never taking his eyes from hers, and in the wise innocence of fourth graders, he said," Why not?"

— *students* —

Matt and I were both teachers in public schools. It never occurred to us that places exist where a community must fight, year after year, to keep a school open for its children.

Courage

The room at the local farm community center is warm on a Saturday morning in November. No, this community center is not a school, though, a mainland official had suggested that we simply use that center for the school. Our island is small, one hundred fifty residents in the wintertime. Approximately ten of those residents are children, four are in the K-5 category. After grade five, students take the ferry to attend another school on the mainland.

The screen is down, shades drawn, computer set up and tables and chairs ready for the Saturday morning meeting, one of many planning meetings with the purpose of trying to save our little island school. The players are the chair person, who is a school committeeman from the mainland; the principal of the mainland middle school, which our students eventually attend; a Town Council member, who is absent from this meeting; and seven islanders: Shawen, Bob, Kate, Allan, Kim, Jen, and I. The mainlanders have come on the 8:00 ferry from the mainland and will leave from the island at 10:30. The tight time schedule forces us to stay on task. Today's meeting will focus on a proposal to move the responsibility for the school building from the town to a not-for-profit agency, one possible way to save money for the town, one possible way to keep our school open.

Bob has created a draft for us to work on. Bullet by bullet we negotiate wording to say what it is we want to say. "Let's not use the word 'permit.' It diminishes us," I say. Someone jokes. "Well, we are in a subservient position, aren't we?" Still, the hopes are high that we can craft a proposal agreeable to the town in this difficult budget year and one that is agreeable to those islanders who want to keep the school for its historic and present day importance in our community and for the sake of our little children.

In the meantime, we were able to keep the school open this year by recruiting volunteers to teach the students and maintain the building. Jen teaches science; her husband Glenn, music; Rosemary, cooking; Ann, health; Pat, art; and Matt, physical education. I teach writing.

On a Monday morning I meet my student for writing instruction. I know him, of course. We live on the island where everyone knows everyone else. He is a third grader, half way between excited, wanting to please, and jumping out of his skin with energy. I love the kid. In just a month and a half he has moved from writing three sentences by hand to writing several paragraphs on computer. He now composes directly on the computer.

Today we begin by talking about what kind of writing he is doing. Always the town binders on educational standards are behind the work. Standards are not a bad thing, I think, as long as they are not prescriptive. While we teachers complain about too much demand for structuring our work, still it reminds each of us what a child might be able to do at a certain learning time in his life.

"Do you remember what kind of writing you are doing now?" I ask.

"Personal narrative," he says, without a pause.

"Why 'personal'?" I ask. "What does that mean?"

"It's about me," he says with a smile.

"What is narrative?"

He's stuck there. So, we go on. He has begun a new writing since I last saw him, one about his science work with Jen. He reads through it and then talks about what he wants to add, about learning that a sponge is an animal.

We go back to the question about narrative. He knows that his writing is about what happened in class, a series of events that occurred. He recognizes that he has story in his writing where there is a turning point, where he expected to touch a wiggly thing in the bag that Jen held out for him, the bag containing an "animal," and his surprise to find that the animal was a sponge.

Vicky, the regular classroom teacher, moves in and out of the room as we work. She answers questions that she thinks we might have.

In all my twenty-eight years as a teacher, I realize I have never been so close to a child's development. Raising my own children was different. I was young. Yes, I taught them, too, and we played and read and created adventures for ourselves. But I was not as obsessed about one facet of their development as I am with my one little student here. What a gift this is for me. Each time I see him, he is different, more academically mature. How can it be, I wonder, that a child would grow that quickly? Now he has introduced the idea of using his writing to explore the subject matter that he learned. This came from him, not me. Ah!

Today my husband Matt prepares for his class in physical education. On this day, he has a kindergartener (a girl), a third grader (a boy) and a fourth grade home-schooled child, sister of the third grade boy. Earlier in the week he had stopped at school to pick up the jump ropes that he had left there for the children. The boy had declined taking a jump rope home the last time Matt was with him. Today, Matt tells him that many of the great athletes of the world jump rope on a daily basis. Before he goes back to the school he wants to adjust the length of the jump ropes for each child.

On this cold, partly cloudy November day he'll take the children for a walk-run, then work with them on jumping rope.

A few weeks before when Matt had taught physical education at the school, he had the children dribbling a soccer ball around cones in the schoolyard. Then they broke up into teams, Matt and the kindergartener on one team, brother and sister on the other. Two-hundred-pound Matt and his tiny kindergarten teammate crouched, hands on knees in a ready position, waiting for the opposing team to bring the ball down the field. The kindergartener turned to Matt and said, "I think I have the courage to do this."

Ah! Courage. Where did she learn this concept of stamina and grit?

All of us on the committee will need strength and courage *to weather the storms* ahead — winter meetings at night on the mainland, weekend meetings on the island, disappointments, agenda after agenda, reviewing, regrouping, appealing — as we continue to try to save our school.

— to weather the storms —

Here's a personal narrative about a literal storm, one of
the many that we have encountered in our years of living on
the island.

Another Storm

"You don't have to pick me up," I said. "I'll stay over."

"Let's play it by ear," Matt said. "If it's not too windy,
I'll come."

Like an old record, we said the same things that we've
said for the past twenty-five years.

High wind warnings had been up for the previous two
days. The ferry ride that morning from the island to the
mainland was the hairiest I've ever experienced. Both Matt
and I trust our boat more than we do the ferry. It's more
maneuverable, less affected by the thrust of the wind.

After a meeting at my friend Jan's house, an hour south
on the mainland, I called Matt at 3:45 p.m. "How does it
look?" I said. "Has the wind diminished?"

"Not bad," he said. When has he ever said "BAD?"
"I'll come to pick up you up. What time can you be at the
dock?"

"5:00 p.m."

"Can you make it by 4:45?"

I knew he was thinking about that tiny window of time
between sunset and darkness. "I'll try."

At 4:50, I pulled into our parking spot in full view of
where Matt would swing the boat into the docking area.
He wasn't there, yet. I decided to stay in the car to wait.
It would take me only a few minutes to walk to the docking
area. Even in the lee of the land, *the fierce wind howled.*

Ah, but it's still light, I thought. I sat happily thinking how great it would be to get home. That's the island condition. We always want to get home to our own beds. I slid out of the car and put on my ski pants, shuffled back inside to wait.

Darkness fell. I still sat in the car. 5:00. 5:15. How long should I wait to call someone. Who would I call? The police? The harbormaster? Matt had the cell phone. I did not.

5:25. Pitch dark and blowing. Oh.

5:30. The running light on the top of the doghouse on our boat showed as it came around the corner. Quickly, I locked the car and hustled around the Fire Station and down to the floating dock.

"The line froze. I had to drop the anchor and put in dry gas. Come on, get in," Matt said, all in one breath.

"Is it wise to go back out?" I asked, noticing how wet and haggard he looked.

"Yeah, it will be all right now. The engine's running fine."

Matt reached out and held my hand as I stepped into the boat. He handed me my foul weather gear. I put my backpack into the dry box and took my place, standing beside him as I snapped up the orange gear.

The wind wasn't fully with us until we rounded the point at the mouth of the harbor, then it hit us, in the two o'clock position of the starboard side.

Every single wave crashed over the boat, soaking us. Matt tried to maneuver each one, though he could hardly see. I held the squeegie and acted as a human windshield wiper, attempting to time my wiping to each wave. Splat! The slushy wave covered the window. Holding tightly with my right hand to the handhold on the doghouse, my left hand shot out to wipe the window. When I missed the timing, I caught a wave right in the face and licked the salty slush from my lips.

The run from the mainland to dock on Harmony Island is only four miles, but on nights like this it feels a lot longer.

The waves were huge. How high? I don't know. Four feet. Five. We've debated the size of waves for years. How does one measure? The wind was blowing maybe thirty miles an hour, maybe forty. What does it matter?

When we were home and warm (I jumped into a hot tub as soon as I got home), we said, once again. Why did we do that? Let's try not to do it again, o.k.?

We agreed. I could have stayed over and come home on the morning ferry. No problem.

— the fierce wind howled —

One day I was walking on the beach where I found a beautiful gull wing.

A Wing on the Beach

On the rocky beach
A drama of feathers lay—
A single wing —
Silver and white
Sweeping to a visual climax,
A seaside Georgia O'Keefe.

The wind ruffled its feathers
And the wing fluttered as though
It might take flight
Might soar from the black beach
But it was a wing with no body
No longer to fly but
To be carried on the whim of the tide.

We are wings without bodies
Caught in black mud of the earth,
Unable to soar like children in dreams
Who fly 'til their wings are clipped.

And we are the children
Whose flesh is still raw
Where wing clung to body.

Is it too late, now, to rejoin
The wing to the body?
Is it enough to know the beauty
Of a wing *on the beach*?

— on the beach —

Simple acts of unselfishness, typified by Marcy's work in the ferry parking lot in front of her store, make living on Harmony Island an extraordinary experience.

Marcy

Marcy is digging shells on the beach when I pull up to the post office. As usual, she wears her red and yellow Mexican-looking jacket. Gray banana curls bob as she drives the flat-edged shovel into the shells.

"What are you doing, Marcy, digging for gold?" I ask. Marcy loves humor.

"No, I'm filling the holes in the parking lot," she says. She keeps her head down and works as she talks. There is no hint of anything except the fact that the holes need to be filled.

I look where my car is parked, and sure enough, the dips in the hard gravel surface are filled with shells. Hole by hole, in front of her store, she is making the parking lot — which she does not own — safer for all of us.

Back in the car on my way to teach at the schoolhouse, I try to figure out how old Marcy is. *Early eighties, I think.* As I drive away, it occurs to me that a neighbor may have sprained his ankle in the lot and Marcy is responding in her usual no-nonsense manner.

—Early eighties, I think —

My elderly friends, Marcy, Bobi, and others, teach me by example what it means to age. For some I rejoice at their mental and physical energy; for others I weep. From each one I learn.

Another Planet

I gasp as Bobi opens the door to her room at the assisted living facility. Beyond her lies a modern-day cave, dimly lit, shades down, sunless. The walls are bare. Nothing meaningful to my friend graces the space, except for a jumble of papers on a desk, probably more letters to her Congressman about the price of gas or the war in Iraq.

She wraps her arms around me. "It's great to see you," she says as she moves around trying to untangle the oxygen bottle. "I'm having a little trouble breathing," she says. "And I can't hear."

Bobi says she's there because she broke some vertebrae in her back. We sit for a while, she on the bed, I in her wheelchair. I make a list of some items she needs from home — a Hawaiian print shirt, a pair of lightweight red slacks — from the post office — ten first class stamps — and from the pharmacy —her special chewing gum with the green wrapper.

Then we walk together down to the cafeteria so she'll be sure to get there without getting lost. She's forgotten where it is. Her walker scrapes along the floor. Along the way she stops, leans against the wall and gasps for breath.

White haired women shuffle along with walkers. I feel as though I'm in a science fiction movie or on another planet. "These are the prisoners," I think. Some folks sit on couches

in the lounge, but no one speaks to another. They simply
sit. We take the elevator down to the cafeteria. The door
opens and a man in a wheelchair, stationed up close, watch-
es, a man who seems far away in his mind, or maybe here
close up, with nothing to do but wait for the opening of the
elevator door.

I leave Bobi at the cafeteria and go off to do errands.
It is hard not to cry as I think of my friend, the treasure
hunter, who was as free as an unbridled pony. She'd jump
into her van and take off for a beach in Virginia. "Want to
come?" she'd say. And off she'd go.

I'm in her home now for sale — around the corner from
my old house where we were neighbors thirty-five years ago —
looking in the closet for the Hawaiian shirt and lightweight
red slacks she asked for. The slacks are not there.

When I return to the place where Bobi now lives, she
tells me that, in two weeks, her daughters are going to take
her to Oklahoma, where she grew up. Can this be possible?
With the oxygen? The pain in her back? "I already have
my plane ticket," she says, "but now there's been a terrorist
problem in England."

I listen.

On the island where I live, I stay close to the elderly
still living at home. They are my friends. Matt and I learn
from them a little of what might be down the road for us.
Our old friend John, in his eighties, lives alone. Hand-
crafted birdhouses, at least a dozen of them, hang from the
low ceiling in his small dark living room. His home is
dark, but it is his. He can choose to be there, or not. His
son Dennis shops for him on the mainland and send his groceries by ferry. Matt cuts his hair, cuts wood for him for the

winter. We share meals with him now and then. We play music with John and listen to his stories, his sadness, his tiredness of being alive, then we strum along as he plays his mandolin with the energy of a man half his age. He laughs when we sing "Be Kind to Your Web-footed Friends." John teaches our friend and her children to play mandolin, and he still works at the transfer station, a hub of activity on the island. He works and strums. These activities keep him alive. He hugs us. And he gives us eggs.

Another neighbor, Pat, lives in her own home on the island. She's eighty-eight. Her hands tremble and she shuffles along with a walker, but her mind is sharp. Pat spends most days lying on the couch reading, indiscriminately, any book she can get her hands on. She lives with arthritis and has recently given in to taking pain medication. Her daughter lives with her and cares for her. Sometimes they play cards or board games. Friends like me call now and then, drop off soup or books, and we talk. "I didn't like the pea soup," she says with a smile. Pat makes an immediate connection with me, talking about the California Redwoods or global warming, something she's read. "Did you know...?" And she goes on. We could talk for hours, but I'm always on my way to somewhere and she may need to lie down again anyway. Maybe a few minutes now and then with a few friends is enough. She says she's lived long enough, yet she seems reasonably content. She has her daughter and other children who visit from Oregon, Massachusetts, and southern Rhode Island.

Tom and Betty are in their eighties. Tom has Alzheimers. Betty cares for him but finds it increasingly difficult as he imagines that he has to walk somewhere, sometimes to the dock a mile away. He looks for a way "to go home." A couple of weeks ago he managed somehow to board the ferry by himself. Serendipitously, their grandson had just begun working as a deckhand. He watched over his grandfather on the return trip to the island. We know they'll need help after the summer. Matt has offered to shovel snow or do whatever physical work needs to be done around the house. I've offered to walk with her husband or sit with him so that Betty can go out or rest. But they also have family, close up, staying in touch, helping.

Marcy is in her eighties, too. Early eighties, I think. She tends the store and receives and sends out the mail. Her life is spent in service to the islanders. Her hands shake a little and so do her gray banana curls, but she remembers that I owe her $4.85, for a package sent a couple of days ago, even as she checks her little filing system of dog-eared envelopes. She works every day from 6:00 a.m. to 7 p.m. or thereabouts. Every day Marcy walks the quarter mile from her house to the store and post office, six times. She's there as the 6:25 a.m. ferry commuters arrive at the dock and at night when the 6:00 p.m. ferry pulls in. She hangs around after the evening commuter ferry for any last minute business at the store.

Marcy and the other islanders are free. My friend Bobi is not. She cannot choose to play a harmonica or stroll down the street. What is a life, alone, with few remnants of the past, with little breath for a sigh or for deep relaxation? How does one exist in a room with four smooth walls, no sunlight, no breath of air, no one to touch or be touched by? Still, she has her children. And she has a plan. Maybe she really will go to Oklahoma.

When I return from my errands, Bobi is on the phone with her son who is a pilot flying all over the world. I forget where he called from, maybe Dubai. She talks with her daughters by phone, too, one in Colorado, the other in Maine. Is that enough? "Sometimes I think there is nothing to live for," she says later.

"You're in pain. It's understandable you'd feel that way," I say. My heart aches for her, alone in her dark room, writing letters to her Congressman.

Just last Thursday, my granddaughter, a beautiful, happy teenager, declared that I am old. "Grandma Grace, you ARE old," she said, giggling. I smiled, then laughed aloud with her, but the comment drove right to the core of my youthful spirit — not in pain, but in a flash of new understanding. I'm a generation younger than Bobi, John, Marcy, Pat, Tom and Betty. I ski, and sing, and walk, and swim, make love, and treasure each moment in my healthy life.

Still, *I pause, now*, thinking of what it is I need to learn.

— I pause now —

Our experiences traveling by boat in what I call a "dead" fog, one where the visibility is zero, inspired me to write this poem and the following short story, "Fog."

This Morning Seth Left Home

This morning Seth left home
    In a dense fog, you know, the kind
        Where you can't see the bow
            From the stern of the boat.

I stood where the land drops off to the sea
    Listening
        To the whine of his engine.

As it died in the distance
        I heard the fog horn's lament,
            Then nothing at all.

For eons I stood there
    Then shuddered —
            And remembered

Your telling me how you shuddered
    The morning Ben died.
        I remember so clearly you told

How you made his bacon and eggs,
    How you called him in,
            And heard no reply.

Then you shuddered and knew
  You would find him
    Beside the old truck
      He was fixing for Rick.

How does that trembling
  Travel through space
    From the ones we love?

I stood at the top of the hill
  Waiting, knowing,
    Then

I heard a man cry.
  He shouted and pleaded
    In the desolate fog.

"I'm sorry, so sorry." He
  Could hardly talk
    For the coughing and wailing.

The sun drew the veil from the sea,
  And I saw him,
    Arms spread like a sinner,
      Pleading for mercy.

"It felt like hitting a wall," he said later.
  "He flew into the air
    And I saw the boat
      Circle 'round the place he went in.
The fog was so thick
Like being in hell."

He is. I am.

—The fog was so thick like being in hell —

I played with point of view and voice in this fictional piece. Ruth is always a composite character, a little bit of me and a lot of fiction. Yes, some of this story is autobiographical — our commuting to our teaching jobs by boat, for example, and our home being close to our neighbor's. This story is told from the perspective of Ruth and Seth's next-door neighbor. The story and the events in it, of course, are fiction. I like blending nonfiction and fiction because it helps me to get inside a story.

Fog

The only reason I decided to write this story of Ruthie and Seth — as if I were telling it to someone sitting here with me — is because I don't know what else to do. I make it a point not to gossip. Who is there to talk to up here at the north end of the island, anyway? Except for Ruthie. And besides, what happened has already happened, and no one can do anything about fog.

A little over five years ago, Ruthie and Seth moved next door to me. Our houses are only fifteen feet apart with that old snow fence between them. Then there are the cedars, two white pines, the dirt road, and the Bay. I like being alone, have been for many years now, but I got used to them being here, though we've never talked much. Seth puttered in the garage and made repairs; Ruth did school work, gardening, and house projects. I could hear their sounds, but they didn't bother me. She sang to the music on her stereo; he thumped on anything he could get

his hands on, a drummer without a drum. Her voice was
soft like a murmur, except when she got excited, then it
sharpened. His sounded more like the bark of a playful
dog. Both of them were friendly enough. Right off the
bat, she made bread for me, and he offered to help with my
firewood.

They were schoolteachers on the mainland, you know,
but it was summer when they moved in, so they weren't
teaching. Some days I'd go out to hang the wash and I'd
see Ruthie *lying on her stomach with her ear to the ground*, like
she thought she'd hear something down there. Other times
she'd be flat on her back with her eyes closed, then she'd
turn over and I could see she was watching a bug. I asked
her once, "What are you doing lying on the ground?" "Oh,
I'm just listening to what's going on down there and I like
to feel the earth next to my body. Sometimes I wish I could
burrow like a vole. Does that sound silly?" I said, "No,"
and I didn't say anything else. I used to do quirky things
like that, too. I still feel the tickles and aches of the earth,
but I'd never met anyone else who did. I didn't tell her because when you're older than seventy, if you tell things like
that people think you're senile, but at thirty, I guess you
can get away with it. I might tell her now that Seth's gone.

Ruthie's a little bit like me in other ways, too, even
though I'm old and she's young. She's small and strong.
Actually, I'm growing smaller, I think, and I know I'm
not as strong as I used to be when I rowed my skiff out to
meet the draggers coming home. For five years Ruthie and
Seth went out in that little boat of theirs, sun and rain, ice
and snow, on their way to school. It was a fiberglass shell
fisherman's boat, open with just a console and a windshield
to block the wind. One day in an awful storm they got
all the way to school and it had been canceled! Imagine!

When Seth had the flu a couple of years ago, Ruthie took the boat to school alone, eight miles to the other side of the Bay, every day for a week. I said to myself, "Good for you, Ruthie."

She liked being out there on wild days. On the worst of them, I'd wait for a chance to hear a story. After dinner she always emptied kitchen scraps at the compost bin. The wind would be blowin' a gale. I'd time it just right and go out to get wood for my fire. The Smith boy down by Homestead cuts for me on the Thulen Farm. My woodpile is just on the other side of her compost bin by the back door. "How was it out there?" I'd say. "Oh, pretty blowy, but the color of the waves," and she'd drift off in the middle of her thought, "the color of the waves make me wish I could paint — the greens and blues — and the way the colors change." She'd say it kind of dreamy like. She seemed so happy. Then she'd be back in the house doing whatever else it is that teachers do at night. Their lights went out early and their house was quiet. I love the quiet of the living at rest, so different from the quiet of the dead.

And sometimes the dead scream.

When Ruthie started teaching at the island school, Seth took the boat to work every day alone. I could tell she worried about him on bad days. She'd be out there — a little person on the hill watching a speck in the distance — til she couldn't see him any more. In snow or fog, she listened for the sound of the engine, as it started up. She knew when the boat had planed off by the steady whine. It's hard when you're not the one in the boat, harder to wait.

I heard her worried voice. It was sharp like mine, — that is, like mine when I used to have somebody to worry about. The morning of the accident I heard their voices outside the front door. Hers was sharp like a coyote's yip, then Seth left for work in that awful fog.

Seth grew up on the island, like his father and his grandfather Ethan, but Seth had gone away to school and hadn't been back to the island for a long time.

Ethan was sweet on me when we were young, but he left the island and married a girl who left him after a couple of years. She ran off with a Newport sailor, leaving Ethan with a toddler. After the child grew up, Ethan came back to marry me. I never asked why he got sidetracked like that. The flame burned hot for both of us. That was enough for me.

And then I lost him.

When I first saw Seth, I gasped. Years and faces got all mixed up and I thought it was Ethan coming back for me. Dark hair. Wind burned face. Handsome. He was a piece of Ethan living next door. Ruth always put out her hand to touch me when we talked — even over the fence. But Seth, when he reached out, I could never touch him, as if I'd burn to a crisp, if I did. And the look in his eye. The crinkles and the blue-green that sparkled.

Seth's whole family were fishermen, his father, his uncles, and his grandfather Ethan. They were part of the sea. They knew its danger, but none of them had what you'd call fear of the sea, any more than they'd fear themselves or each other. Seth, he had a shell fisherman's boat, but he wouldn't be a fisherman. Instead he taught children about jellyfish, about striped bass, blue crabs, and harbor seals, and about wind and tides — and fog. He told me one day that he wanted to teach his students to keep the sea and its creatures safe. He didn't like the big rigs, like the draggers. Maybe, — and I don't know this for sure, — maybe after he heard the story of his grandfather, my Ethan, he figured they were too dangerous.

The day of that awful fog, I knew Ruthie would beg Seth not to go to work in the boat and I knew he would go. There's no saying who's right and who's wrong.

We don't usually have fog in February, but there it was. That morning from my bathroom window I saw Ruthie sitting on that bench over there, on the rise that runs down to the water. She had her face set toward the upper Bay, and she had her arms wrapped around in her brown shawl, hugging herself, like she was holding body and soul together. I didn't dare go out. I felt shaky and kind of sick. It was cold and you couldn't see a thing, not even the moorings in front of our houses, a couple of hundred feet out. She should have been getting ready for school. She teaches the little ones on the island. I knew she was listening for Seth's outboard. Sound travels a long way in the fog.

She told me later she heard Seth's engine roar away from Toledo's Dock, down the way. And she heard its whine in the distance. Then she said she heard a crack, like a shot from a gun! And a shout! That's all she said.

And, of course, everyone knows the rest.

Last Friday night my bedroom window was open a crack and so was hers. It was four in the morning, very dark and still, and I was listening to the Great Horned Owl in the big white pine, trying to hear whether it was the male or the female, calling. Then I heard a shriek like a woman in awful labor with a child coming hard, but I knew Ruthie was not having a child.

Then Ethan's last day and my own pain came flooding back just as it has so many times before.

It is a pink and blue mirror calm morning in late December, just before the holidays. The sun is still below the horizon. The pinks and blues reflect off the water through a haze like a gauzy blanket. Ethan hums as he finishes dressing, and he picks up his gear. He loves these trips beyond the Bay to the edge of the Atlantic, especially on such magical mornings. His blue green eyes sparkle. We look right at each other as he kisses me good-bye.

As in a dream he rows out in the little wooden dinghy, barely big enough for his bulk, a giant in a toy boat, pulling the oars together, creating his own rhythm. Then he loses his color in the haze and becomes a silhouette in motion. I cannot see him climb aboard the dragger, and I shiver, tremble really, thinking I'm coming down with the flu.

For me — except for feeling sick — this is a beautiful memory that plays as clearly today as it did fifty years ago. If it were only this scene, I could be at peace. If it were the sea that he loved that had taken him. But my imagination is stronger and I hear his screams. He is caught in the dragger hoist, both arms. He goes round the hoist gears, crushing and bleeding as the crew tries frantically to close it down, but the machine eats him up and what is left is not Ethan, but a mass of blood and flesh.

I know Ruth's shout, because I have shouted like that so many times at that desperate hour before dawn.

So when it was light and I knew she'd be up, I went around the snow fence and knocked on her door. She seemed to know I'd be there and she invited me in for tea. The little round table by the window facing the Bay was already set with two cups, just like mine used to be after

Ethan's death when I hoped somebody would come in. She
poured the tea from her brown porcelain pot and sat across
from me, holding her cup as if her hands were cold. Her
eyes were dark and ringed with pain and lack of sleep.
I wasn't sure if I should say Seth's name. We talked about
the ice that's moving down the bay and about seeds. We
both order seeds in the thick of winter. It's a way to bring
spring home sooner.

—lying on her stomach with an ear to the ground —

Have you ever tried lying on the ground like this?
I did. As children, we probably all did.

Still

With an ear to the ground
She heard thunder
Far away, beyond the hill
She lay upon

Still as stone, she saw
The sun
A radiant dandelion
An inch from her eye
And watched a robin
Beat his feet
And heard, and heard
The worm!

The robin
Pecked then pulled,
Pulled on the worm until
It stretched longer than any worm
Could be.

She closed her eyes and
Felt *the rhythm*
Of the earth
Her own heart
The growing grass.

— the rhythm of the earth —

Set on the island where we live, the following fictional piece incorporates memories and moments from the real past intermingled with the imagined characters of Ruth and Til, who appear again later in this collection.

Til

Til lives. At the north end of the island. Beyond the gate. Where there are no houses.

"I know she lives there. Everyone on the island knows." Ruth finds herself talking out loud as she walks toward the gate that marks the Harmony Island boundary between private and public land, the land set aside as a sanctuary to protect the endangered.

Anyone on the island will tell you that Til is beautiful, though no one is sure of her age. Her hat woven from cedar boughs protects her face from the sun and her skirt of golden switch grass catches the light. As she ducks under the gate, Ruth catches a glint of light and thinks it might be Til, but when she straightens up, only the empty path rolls out before her.

Dying happens more often on the island than anywhere else, she thinks. Of course, that is only partially true. Birth and death happen everywhere, but on the island births are rare. The older folks outnumber the younger. Only a few little kids attend the island school. Another dozen older kids commute by ferry to school on the mainland. So, there are young families, but... Maybe, it's that the community is small, so everyone feels each death more acutely.

Ruth walks on in a swirl of memories. She and Seth and their island neighbors have worked on rescues and known trauma and tragedy, close up. She remembers doing mouth-to-mouth resuscitation on a dying hunter, holding the blistered hand of a man burned in a gas explosion, sitting with an elderly friend as she drew her last breath. It is the way of the island. Neighbors tend to neighbors. And always, when someone dies, Ruth has felt that a little of herself dies, too. That is the price of commitment, she thinks. And so on this wonderful island, she lives in the paradoxical state of exquisite joy clamped firmly to sadness and melancholy that comes with loss.

She walks in a steady rhythm like a drum beat along the path. Ruth and Seth. Ruth and Seth. They moved to the island five years ago. Both felt they had come home. Upclose living. Life and death. A rustle in the brush intrudes on her thoughts. "Til?" She whispers. A snort and flash of a white tail announce another woodland creature. A deer leaps across the path and disappears through a hole in the wall of briars.

Everyone says Til knows about death. Island stories, depending whose version you hear, tell of the death of Til's parents in a raging fire at the north end of the island where they had lived in her grandmother's ancestral home. Another version of her story tells of Til's parents, financially ruined on the mainland during the Great Depression. Too poor to raise their five children and reluctant to send them to an orphanage, the parents dropped off the children from a skiff onto the island at the north end, where there was an abandoned farm house. Some of the older folks on the island, like Andy at the stone dock store, said his mother vaguely remembered the kids. They attended the island school for a while, but then an accident happened and the house burned. Til survived, but no one could catch and tame the pubescent sprite. She joined the subtle, shy world of the island coyote and the indigo bunting.

According to island lore, Til became a gatherer in the oldest tradition, eating wild asparagus at the northern tip of the island, plantain, acorns and black walnut, berries, wild pear, cherries, and apples. It is said that she ate wild carrot and the roots of Burdock and that she made teas from blackberry leaves and roots, from St. John's Wort and other herbs. Islanders say that Til lives and that she knows about death and survival, but Ruth wonders how she exists through desolate winters.

Now it is April, almost three months after Seth's death, and a hard and painful time on the island. Everyone looks for warmth and growth, but the air is damp and cold and the leaves have yet to unfurl. Hardly a hint of life provides evidence of survival. Last year's milkweed pods hang like great teardrops on gray stalks. Blackberry brambles with tearing thorns reach spiked fingers into the path. Bare branches of oaks groan as they rub each other raw.

On Harmony Island Ruth has friends of all ages, but she has no immediate family nearby. She thinks she needs Til, or someone like Til. A healer. Ruth's mother died years ago of bronchial cancer. Her mother-in-law, beloved of Ruth like the Biblical Naomi, perished with her husband about a year ago in an automobile collision. Even after losing these women in her life, Ruth does not yet know that the pain of birth and the experience of death must be borne and embraced alone. Her next-door neighbor — her only neighbor at the north end — and other islanders have come to console her, but she has felt distant from them, isolated and disconnected.

Ruth turns right at the crossroads toward the Cove. At the store, Ruth's friend Andy had told her about a field of Roman chamomile Til had planted years ago. He tried to explain to her where it is. He said it might help to calm her mind. Others have told of lying peacefully in Til's field of chamomile. But it's too early for chamomile blossoms, and she's not sure she'd recognize the plant without the flower. She turns back toward the main path and searches for new growth as she heads north again looking for Til.

The elm at Cedar Hill stands bare, branches uplifted as if for the last time. It is a big old survivor barely hanging on now. She wades through the strange sandy spot along the path, the spot that seems like beach sand. The grasses are brown and gold, but Ruth notices only the mud beyond the sand, her head down, washed by a wave of sadness as she thinks of Seth.

According to the sobbing fisherman whose boat struck Seth's in a February fog, Seth flew out of the boat and slipped out of sight. From her bench at the top of the embankment, Ruth sat with her binoculars and watched for days as boats circled the area. Islanders and mainland fishermen participated in the search, but Seth never resurfaced.

Ruth grew up ten miles north of where she now lives on Harmony Island. In the small beach community of her childhood, most people came with cars bursting with bouncing kids and wag-tailed dogs, beach pails and bright summer clothes, to stay the summer and return to city homes in the winter.

Each September the yellow Ryder school bus rumbled
into the turnaround near Cauldron's store. The door
clapped open, and the bus driver, gray-haired and wrinkly
like her grandfather Pépé, said with a twinkle in his eye,
"O.K., you clam diggers, all aboard." Ruth in her dark auburn pig-tails, broke into a toothy smile and climbed into
the bus along with the rest of the year 'round kids.

After school and on weekends she and her friends squatted in the mud watching for fiddler crabs or waded ankle
deep in water thick with seaweed to net blue claw crabs.
While all her friends loved the game of netting crabs, only
Ruth and her buddy Riley ate them. They steamed all
the crabs on the beach stone fireplace in Ruth's back yard
and feasted on the group's catch. Other days they hunted
for clams, giggling as they stamped around in the black
mud and watched for squirts that signaled the place to dig.
Ruth's father routinely dug for steamers and caught a crab
or two in his net. Her mother prepared steamers and qua-
hog chowder, a feast for all the neighborhood kids.

When it was too cold for clamming and crabbing,
Ruth's father took her and her sister frost fishing with
spears at night. Fish flapped where the waves rippled onto
the sand. They took home an easy catch. During the day
in the dead of winter, friends played on ice floes that piled
up like beached rafts along the shore, and they skated in the
cove when the salt ice hardened enough to support them.

Ruth sometimes felt like a fish, not the frost fish that
flapped at the water's edge, but a fish that swam comfortably and gracefully in the sea. One summer day when she
was seventeen, Cathy, a school friend who had been racing
sail boats from the time she was a little girl, invited Ruth
to go sailing. Though Ruth had lived by the water all her

life, she had never sailed. "What if we tip over?" She asked. "What should we do?"

Cathy laughed, "I've been sailing for ten years," she said. "I tipped over the first summer when I was seven, but not since then. I remember our instructor telling me to stand on the keel and try to right the boat. It worked on my tiny sailboat. Ruth, if you and I tip over, we'd try to do that, but we might not be able to pull the boat up because this is a heavy cat boat and we are both lightweights. We'd wave someone down for help."

On the way back into the harbor, the catboat heeled over in the wind. The sheet caught something sticking out of the water and the boat flipped before they knew what was happening.

Ruth did not know she had been struck across the bridge of the nose by the boom. Under water the world moved like a lullaby. Slowly Ruth rose to the surface under the sail. To take a breath she tried to lift the sail, but it sucked tightly to the water. She dove down and felt like a fish swimming through thick water, as though she could breathe. But as she prepared to inhale deeply, a little signal beeped in her brain. She held off and glided beyond the sail and up to the surface. Like a fish, she thrived in thick, salty water. When she popped through the surface and saw Cathy straddling the overturned hull, the world seemed alien, moving too fast, like a song played at high speed.

Ruth had thought that somehow Seth would rise to the surface as she had, that he'd surprise them all. When he didn't, she wished she had drowned with him.

Eventually Ruth comes to the old cellar hole at the former North Farm. She looks into the hole imagining that Til might actually live down there. Oak and maple leaves lie banked against one side. The walls remain intact, stone upon stone, unmoved for a hundred years. Where can Til live? That's the thing that has always bothered Ruth about the stories of Til. The north end of the island is a small area, only seven hundred fifty acres. Thick briars and tangles of blackberry brambles — and the infamous deer tick — make exploring off the paths nearly impossible, but certainly after all these years, someone must have discovered her dwelling — or maybe no one has wanted to break the spell cast by Til's possibility.

"Til," she calls out. "Til, can you hear me?" A breeze ruffles a cedar and for a second Ruth is sure that it is Til, her cedar bough hat caught by the stirring wind, her voice humming like the sound of the earth in motion.

Ruth turns around in place wondering which way to go. She steps off to the right again down a path she does not know. The ground is more solid under foot. Without thinking, she snaps a branch from a bush, but when she chews it she spits out the wad and tosses the branch aside. She snaps another. Her eyes scan mosses and grasses, whatever is at her feet.

Before she set out for her walk to the north end of the island, Ruth did not ask anyone exactly how she would find Til. She just knew from stories — especially from those who had been desperate — that when you really needed Til, she'd be there. Like God, according to those who believe. And so rather naively, she now thinks, she had set forth, looking for Til, with the assurance that she was there to be found.

Now she wonders. Had she every really spoken to anyone who had met with Til? Who had been healed by her? She comes to an opening in the trees where she sets her backpack down and lowers herself to the ground to think — and to eat her lunch. She pulls her sandwich of hummus and greens from the backpack, lays it on the carpet of soft green and unscrews the cap of her thermos of chamomile, her favorite calming tea.

Ruth closes her eyes and chews slowly, wondering all the while exactly what healing means. She calls out in a somewhat strident voice, as if to question the briars and brambles. "How can I live without Seth? How can I find you, Til?" Foliage absorbs the sound of her voice.

The afternoon sun warms her back and she swivels around, to lift her face, eyes closed, to bathe in the cool warmth of the late April sun. She finishes her sandwich, takes the last sip of tea, sets the thermos on the ground, and lies back with the sun full on her. And there she slips into a dreamy state.

During so many nights over the past few months as she has lain in a half sleeping state, Ruth has felt her bed move, as though Seth were turning in his sleep. She has reached over to touch him. Finding him gone, she has cried in her sleep and awakened to heaving sobs. Alone in her bed she has allowed the wrenching spasms and shouts to wrack her body until she is exhausted.

The bed has moved. She knows it.

Now she smiles in her dreamy state, remembering how silly Seth was when he was getting into bed. Sometimes he was a great soft gorilla. He'd scratch his belly and make ape sounds. Sometimes he was a goat with horns. He'd dive at her until they were laughing and tossing in sexual play in the nest of their bed. To her surprise she is smiling now as she remembers Seth and thinks about how funny he

was and about the bed and how it moves. Eyes closed she
puts her hands to her mouth to trace her own smile.

And now she feels a firm hand on her abdomen and
another under her back. She hears a keening, high pitched
and ethereal, and then a low *humming like the sound of the
earth in motion.* While she wants to move, she dares not, nor
can she open her eyes. Ruth has no idea of the passage of
time. It is only when the hands move to hers, when they
enclosed her hands like warm earth embracing the bean
seed, that she has the courage to open her eyes. And there
is Til, bending over her, dark clear eyes, tawny skin, that
beautiful face framed by the cedar bough hat. Til. Ruth
smiles and closes her eyes again. She stretches out and
sleeps.

When she awakens, she finds beside her on the ground
a small bough of the shadbush, its delicate white petaled
flowers and soft serrated leaves testimony to Til's presence,
she thinks. But would Til ever snap a bough? It is said
that she moves without leaving a footprint, without bending a blade of grass.

Ruth sits cross-legged while she packs up her lunch bag
and thermos in the backpack. She breathes deeply and rubs
her hands over the ground, suddenly aware that this could
be the bed of chamomile. Ruth rises effortlessly from her
sitting position, stands, hoists her backpack onto her back,
and heads down the path toward the gate. To the right and
leaning over the path is the shadbush fully dressed in white
blossoms and their promise of fruit. How could I have
missed this before? She thinks. The way ahead is fluo-
rescent watery green, striped by the brown walking path.
Fronds of golden switch grass glow in the westering sun.

Further on, long shadows shade the path through the woods. Ruth focuses on each step through the springtime mud. At the clearing near Cedar Hill she stops. She knows no sound has occurred but for the squish of her footsteps. Yet she has distinctly heard a voice. A silent voice? She turns to her right and sees again the old elm, its trunk and main branches devoid of much of its life-giving bark, but with its arms uplifted, silhouetted against the western sun – as if in celebration.

For a long time she stands, holding the flowering shad-bush in her hand, and considers the tree. Thick limbs beginning at the trunk opens upward, a gilt fan against a blue silk sky. A smile turns the corners of her mouth. In the fading light of day she walks the rest of the way home in a world vibrant with brilliant grass greens and the haze of red hovering over the budding maples, the flash of cardinal's red, and the honk of Canada geese overhead.

The next morning in her bed by the window, the bed that has again moved during the night, Ruth lies with her eyes closed, listening to morning sounds and waiting for the light. The pillow feels soft on her cheek, and she cradles her head there for a while.

When she opens her eyes, white light from the rising sun bathes herring gulls that float on the updraft from the embankment in front of the house. Their underbellies reflect pearly pink from the water. Thin yellow legs stretch back under their tails. Wave tips pick up the frothing light and gull wings flutter like so many messages dropping onto the dark sea.

She rolls out of bed, slips her feet into her slippers, and scuffs toward her bureau, which holds the underwear, shirt and jeans that she will wear this day. She stops to stretch, reaching her hands to the sky, and she gasps, stunned. In the shell mirror on the wall, she now sees, as if for the first time, her own dark eyes, auburn hair and beautiful tawny skin.

— humming like the sound of the earth in motion —

For me, some moments are like tiny isolated crystals of time.

Face down

Face down
In soft sand
The sea otter lies

On a Calm Sea

On a calm sea
Thin-necked grebes
Slice through glass

—*face down* —

I wrote this personal narrative so that we could remember our friend John. Even as I reread it, my throat tightens.

John

All day I felt a deep melancholy. What is it? I thought. My body feels good, hips, back, belly. What's going on? Cate, my acupuncturist, said that late August is a time of melancholy, the time of the lung.

"You're right on target," she said.

"I'm glad to be tuned into the larger rhythms," I said.

The melancholy hung on, as I drove from her office to meet Matt, where he was working with Mattie. I didn't think I could face anyone. This is not the "normal" me. In the breakdown lane (hmm), I dialed up my friend Jan. I'm not much of a phone talker, but I felt almost desperate to connect with someone. No answer. Jane Sylvia, both her numbers. No answer.

I hadn't talked with my old friend Amelia in a few years. With her I had swum the bay three times, almost thirty years ago, had skied in Austria with her and my children when I was struggling as a single parent. How old must she be? 86? I dialed her up. Her phone was no longer in service and I felt a punch in the gut. Maybe she's dead, I thought.

Next I tried my daughter Laurie and talked with her husband about his French, his project on the house, the workshops he had run on the weekend.

After talking with Jim, though I didn't say anything about my melancholy, I felt better and continued on my way to Matt and Rachel's house.

Later that night after a lovely boat ride over satiny water, we met a neighbor walking in the darkness with her granddaughter. "Did you know that Mr. Canario died today?" she asked. Her voice sounded like an echo, an otherworldly sound saying something I could not comprehend.

"No, we didn't know that," I said.

"He didn't go to work at the dump today. One of the town workers went to his house and found him, face down on the floor of his living room."

Neither Matt nor I could talk on the way home.

Two days before, on Tuesday, we played music at our house with John and other members of our group. He laughed when we played *Down in the Valley*, Ted and Allison playing melody, Malcolm calling out the words, Cynthia and I singing louder and with more complex harmony as we progressed through the song, Matt on bass, Glenn strumming along. John loved to hear us sing loud and that night when we sang for him, he turned his face toward me and laughed. That night, too, he praised Cynthia for doing a good job on a song, an unusual thing for him to do. He congratulated Matt on doing a "wonderful job" singing "Are You Lonesome Tonight."

Talking on music night irritated John. We were there to play music. When we talked between songs, his fingers never stopped. Recently he played, over and over, bits of the latest song that he wanted me to learn, "La Vie en Rose." He commonly introduced new songs by this method of osmosis. That night, however, I rubbed his back with my left hand, while we talked as a group about some issue. He remained quiet and mellow.

At the end of the session when he was ready to leave, I gave John a hug. He told me about a hands-on healer he had seen on television and he said, "You really do have healing hands, Grace." Those were the last words he said to me.

Wednesday afternoon close to four o'clock, with my car windows down, I drove to the post office. As I passed the street where John lived, I heard John playing for the community, as he did practically every night, his windows open, his mandolin plugged into loud speakers.

That last afternoon, the song I heard him play was, of course, *La Vie en Rose.* "O.K., John, O.K., I'll learn it," I say.

He died either Wednesday night or Thursday morning.

Matt and I sat at dinner the night after Cheryl had met us in the darkness. We listened to CD's of John's music, recorded at various performances over the years and we talked about what we'd remember about him —

- his bringing a newborn fawn to our house for me to take its photo with him
- his coming into the house for dinner with knees bloodied after falling on the west side rocks as he tried to extricate a trapped yearling
- his putting a band aid on a wounded snake
- his calling the men handsome and his telling the women they should be nuns
- his saying what a wonderful family Matt and I had, how wonderful his sister, how great my daughter
- his saying we were his best friends
- his repeating over and over that I was intelligent and beautiful and….he'd get stuck with what to say next
- his saying how much he appreciated our helping him, the meals, Matt's cutting his hair and supplying him with firewood for the winter.

John made us — and others — feel good. The men were all handsome and the women beautiful. He kissed their hands at the transfer station. "You're number one," he'd say to one brother. To the other, "You're number two." Then he'd switch if number two did something praiseworthy. When Matt cooked the breakfast on Sunday morning, John said, "You're number one, Matt. Can I eat now?" And he'd laugh.

On a Saturday in September, a few weeks after his death, we held A Celebration for John Canario at the community center on the island. There we heard those kinds of stories, over and over again. One hundred fifty to two hundred people — our *community* — came to laugh and cry, to break bread together, to listen to the music that John was part of, and to tell their stories — to share in the celebration of who he was and still is in our hearts.

— *community* —

The writing of this personal narrative is my way of saying thank you to the rescue team on Harmony Island.

Rescue

On September 11, 2001 an attack on the World Trade Center devastated multiple communities: geographical communities, professional and business communities, family communities, police, fire and rescue communities, in essence, the world community. All individuals connect, especially in times of crisis.

Recently, while visiting friends in Manhattan, we saw the movie "World Trade Center." The suffering, particularly of two trapped firemen, was heart wrenching, as was all the suffering portrayed in the film. What surprised me most, however, was that Oliver Stone succeeded in showing not only a graphic account of suffering during and after the 9/11 attack but also a story raised up from one of suffering to one of celebration. One of the final scenes showed the first of the two firemen, trapped below twenty feet of rubble, strapped in a stretcher and rising up out of the rubble. Above the smoking pile, the stretcher passed along a double column of firemen in full fire fighting gear, their hands held high as though they were carrying a king, five hundred individuals, passing along a survivor among them, in a celebratory gesture of unity.

The two men had been trapped twenty feet below the surface, under slabs of concrete that had fallen in on them as they themselves tried to rescue others. Like all of us, they were isolated from the rest of the world. No one knew they were there. They were separated from each other, each trapped in his own unit of pain. One could not see the other, but they could call out to offer each other support. And one of them could reach up with a great deal of effort to clang a pipe against stone to try to communicate to someone somewhere who might hear.

Isolation and community. Two men isolated. Alone. But together. Apart, but part of something larger than themselves. Men in excruciating pain. Men with hope. Through the huge story of a nation's disaster, this story spoke about our every day lives.

My every day life, for example. I couldn't help remembering an incident that happened to me last October.

While my life, like the larger life in the city of New York, hums along busily and rather peacefully, a surprise attack of major proportions occurred. During late September, within a week's time, two different individuals attacked me verbally, striking right at my heart. Emotional pain invaded my body and produced a strong physical reaction. The tower of my being collapsed in excruciating pain, which drove deeper and deeper into my body. I was frightened, trapped by pain, unable to extricate myself. At last, early on a stormy morning during a driving rain, I called 911.

For ten years my husband Matt and I had been Emergency Medical Technicians in our community. Time after time we responded to 911 calls and each time had tended to individuals in need. This was the first time, however, that I had needed that kind of assistance, and it was the time I would learn how precious a community of neighbors can be to an individual isolated by pain.

In came the EMT's and their assistants — my neighbors and friends. They strapped me into the stretcher, handling me gently, careful not to jostle, not to increase my pain. I felt cared for. When they raised up the stretcher I felt like a queen. Even while I was experiencing the worst pain I could ever remember in my life, I felt euphoric. My community. Ah!

In the rescue vehicle as I drifted in and out of awareness of my surroundings, the hand of one first responder was always on my shoulder. A hand that was solid, reassuring, unmoving. Support in the swirling fog of pain. The rescuers in both the large canvas of the World Trade Center story and in my smaller community linked those isolated in pain to the possibility of the embrace that would heal.

The World Trade Center incident, along with both the pain and the celebration of community, loom large on the canvas of human happenings. The comparatively small attack on me and the rescue by my local community rescue team are a speck in that universe. Yet in each case the movement from isolation and pain to the embrace by a community of peers is testimony to heroism and to joy in the midst of suffering in ordinary life.

— Isolation and community —

This personal narrative tells of another incident on Harmony Island, where the community comes together for the sake of an individual, this time for one who is lost.

Search

"Oh, Happy New Year!" I said to the soft voice on the telephone. It was Ann. I hadn't seen her over the holidays. Like so many of our neighbors on the rural island, where we live, Ann is a friend and a dedicated community worker.

"I'm sorry to say this, Grace, but we need volunteers to search for Tom. He's missing. Volunteers are gathering mid-island at the Hill."

Tom was a gentle man, small in stature, stooped with age. He and his wife Betty, a nurse by profession, lived mid-island adjacent to the property known as the Hill. Both were in their eighties. Tom had been diagnosed with Alzheimers more than ten years earlier. Dedicated and competent, Betty had cared for him at home. During the summer months, Betty's brother Buzzie and other family members helped with Tom's care. We islanders hovered around and provided support for Betty. An artist might have depicted us as a primitive village with straw huts, villagers swaying, humming, offering our hands and our prayers.

Recently, Tom may have suffered from pneumonia. The doctors believed that decreased oxygen going to his brain had affected his mental acuity. When Tom wandered away onto the ferry that day a few weeks earlier, his grandson, now a deckhand, contacted Betty and escorted his grandfather home.

"O.K.," I said to Ann on the phone. "I'll be right there." It was about 4:30 and almost dark on this January late afternoon. Images of Tom wandering, cold and confused, swept across my mind.

My husband Matt was out walking. Salmon sat thawing on the counter for dinner. Our music group would be gathering in a couple of hours, eight of us, who hadn't played since our early December performance. I was moving fast now, preparing to put our lives on hold in order to join our community in the search for Tom.

In the upstairs room where we play music, I turned on the lights, including the light that shines on the back door. On that door I taped a big sign. "Come on in. Play some music. We may be back soon. Or not." A sense of urgency rose up inside me and it didn't occur to me to write, "Come join the search." I wasn't thinking clearly. Tom was missing and it was almost dark.

On the table I scribbled a note for Matt, telling him about the search. "I'll see you there," I wrote. I grabbed the cell phone and my favorite flashlight and drove off down the dirt road toward the Hill, two miles away. I flicked on the high beams to see the potholes better and suddenly saw in my mind the note I had written to Matt. Maybe our music friends will see that note and join the search, I thought, or maybe Ann called them, too.

A mile or so down the road near the center of the island, I saw Matt walking toward home. "Come on, get in," I said. "Tom is missing."

"I know," he said. "Dick drove by on the search."

It was fully dark now, and the scene at the Hill looked like a modern day wagon train, circled around. Fire and rescue vehicles trained lights and spotlights on the center, which created a gathering place for neighbors, young and old, who arrived singly or in pairs, each individual finding a way into this community event. Our fire chief stood by the trucks.

"Report in to Glenn," Bob repeated over and over, as friends and neighbors, including those in our musical group, arrived on the scene. Bob is our EMT captain and a community leader, grounded like the strongest of our oaks.

Each new arrival stepped forward to Glenn, our young island policeman. Each gave a name and number of a cell phone. "Do you have a flashlight?" he asked each one. In the eerie glow of headlights, he stood, end of the day stubble on his square chin, efficiently recording answers to his questions.

We milled around, chatting with neighbors, until Bob announced that we would form teams of eight, each of us with an experienced person — a fire fighter, island police, former island police, anyone with experience. Each team had a defined "neighborhood" to cover.

Tom and Betty's home near the Hill lies adjacent to a heavily wooded area. During the early part of the search, I heard no one say anything about the woods, though our fire chief may have already made arrangements for dogs to search there later, if need be. Two nights earlier Tom had wandered into a neighbor's cellar at three in the morning. The previous night, a lost hunter had been found, dead, only two hundred yards from his own home. The community was tired; they had already suffered a loss. The search focused on nearby houses where Tom might huddle to keep safe and warm.

The night was black and cold, but not bitterly cold as it can sometimes be in January. Later someone said there had been a full moon, but I remember feeling the blackness of the night. Crisscrossing lights slashed through darkness and

turned familiar neighborhoods into strange places.
At every house we tried doors, looked under porches,
opened woodsheds, and called "Tom, hey, Tom." Where a
door was unlocked, we entered homes, those abandoned for
the winter, those used by hunters but with no one home at
the time, and we searched under beds, in closets, in every
nook and cranny of a house, calling, "Tom!"

Strange that a neighborhood looks so different in the
dark during a search! A home is not so-and-so's house; it is
a locked or unlocked house. It is not a lovely newly deco-
rated home or an older summer-type cottage; it is simply a
place where Tom might be — or not.

"I've checked that one," someone shouted.

"What about this one?"

"No."

"That one's locked."

"O.K."

"We're finished. Let's go back."

In the darkness the eight of us climbed up to the gravel
road and walked south, back to the Hill, where each team
checked in.

It was nearly 8:00 p.m. "We're going to move the
search center to the Fire Station," the Chief said. "We're
waiting for the search dogs, then we'll reorganize our
searchers."

Back in the car Matt and I drove along silently, heading
south toward the Fire Station. I was hungry.

"What do you think?" I said. I knew that in order to
continue to think clearly I'd have to eat soon.

"It's going to be long," he said.

"Do you want to quit?" I said, knowing that I had used
a loaded word.

"No."

We were almost at the fire station south of mid-island. "Neither do I," I said. "What do you think about going home and eating quickly? We might be at the Station until 11:00 o'clock or later — maybe all night. We knew the search would continue until Tom was found.

Balancing Catholic guilt with personal necessity, I turned the car around and headed north toward home. I remembered learning as an EMT that we have to protect ourselves before we can help others. The salmon broiled quickly and we spooned out rice, onions, mushrooms, and garlic along with sweet potatoes that I had made earlier. I wondered what others were doing about eating or about taking care of personal needs that go on even when there is a crisis to attend to. Nearly everyone on the island was involved in the search.

We shoveled down our meal and forty-five minutes later were back at the station, standing among waiting volunteers. Shortly, the chief emerged from the station and said, "We're going to break up now and let the search dogs do their thing." Apparently during the search for a missing person, the search dogs become confused when there are too many conflicting human scents. Bob, Glenn, and two young island men would assist with the search in the woods they know so well.

"We'll call on the minitones if we need you to come back," said the Chief. After twenty years as members of the fire department, ten of those as Emergency Medical Technicians, Matt and I no longer had the emergency signal devices. Glenn said he'd call us.

We headed home, talking together about Betty and what it must be like for her. Her daughter had come to the island from another state to comfort her mother. They and the island — and Tom, wherever he was — waited.

Matt felt certain that the search dogs would do what we could not do, that is, sniff out Tom, if he were in the woods. Our teams had searched all of the surrounding homes, and he was not there. So, on Friday morning, Matt left at seven to run some errands on the mainland. I got up to make bread for our planned lunch with friends. I was tired from searching for Tom in my mind all night, so I made bread dough and contrary to my usual "shot out of a cannon" beginning of the day, I lay back down for an hour, certain that Tom must have been found by now.

When I got up, I cleaned my teeth and moved through my morning routine, then checked for phone messages. There was another message from Ann. "We're reorganizing the search," she said. That had been at 8:30. Why had I not heard the phone? It was already 9:00 a.m.

I grabbed my cereal, half finished in the bowl, poured my tea into a travel mug of Matt's. With a sigh, I looked at my rising bread dough and went off to the Fire Station, where, once again, neighbors gathered.

Our community had widened. Firefighters and police from four mainland towns joined us. Search dogs were penned in the back of state police vehicles. Tom was still out there, somewhere. I pictured him seated against a tree, hugging his knees, confused. He had been missing for eighteen hours.

Our larger community now included a mainland hospital, which sent food for volunteers on the morning ferry. Muffins and sandwiches sat on tables in the fire truck bays for those of us who milled around waiting for instructions.

Cynthia was there. Her professional practice revolves around the Wisdom Wheel and Native American spirituality. I said, "I've been thinking that it's too bad we don't have a seer in the community." I knew I could say that to her because the nature of her thinking and her spiritual practice. She might even be a douser.

Even as I spoke, it occurred to me that if I had a pendulum and a map I might be able to locate Tom. I wondered what we could use as a pendulum. A flood of uncommon energy swept though me. Out loud I said, "Maybe I could try dousing."

George was sitting next to me, George as conservative looking as any mainland engineer or businessman, our friend George, also a spiritual man. "I'm glad I'm not the only one thinking like that," he said. He pulled out a ring of keys. We took one key off it and tied it to a string. Then I raced over to the table where I saw maps of the center of the island near a policeman at the front table. "May I?"

"Sure," and he handed one to me.

George, Cynthia, and the others on our new search team started for the lighthouse, just down the hill from the fire station. We were to search the houses and the brush along the beach. I ducked away from the group and knelt behind my car on the grass along the road. I tried to use the key and the map to douse Tom's spot quickly, but the key was too big for the map and my heart was beating fast. Someone yelled, "Are you O.K.? Do you have a flat tire?"

"Thanks, I'm fine," I said, not wanting to call attention to myself, and I went to join the others in the back of Sharon's truck for a ride down the hill.

At the bottom of the hill near the dock, I decided to go up to Nanda's apartment to see if she had a pendulum. Nanda teaches yoga on the island and she has vast experience in places from India to Tennessee. Maybe she could find Tom on the map. "I'll catch up with you down the beach," I said to my group.

"Nanda," I shouted from inside the door. "Nanda."
I knew I might be waking her. "We need your help."

"Come on up, Grace," she said, and met me at the top
of the stairs in her nightgown.

"You know Tom is missing. Do you have a pendulum?"

Time slowed down inside Nanda's apartment. Among
the myriad papers and threads, she pulled a string. "Go to
that window," she said, softly. "The energy is good there.
I'll find something and I'll make you a cup of tea."

I thought of my team of companions searching the
beach, then I realized that Nanda and I would be searching,
too, in our way. "Relax," I said to myself. I knelt on the
floor in the sunshine with the map before me, bent over it
with my eyes closed, and breathed until my heart slowed to
normal. "How does one search?" I asked myself.

Nanda rustled behind me. She handed over a cup of
dark tea and threaded a bead onto a cord. "I think this is
too light," she said. I held it.

"No, it'll work," I said.

"Do you want to try it?"

"You try first."

Over the map I bent, talking to Tom, asking him if
this was the place, or that. The pendulum swung back and
forth, back and forth, then round and round. I got a posi-
tive reading at the beach at the end of Broadway, but it felt
counter intuitive.

Broad Street is a wide road and the only one running
east-west across the island. It is south of Tom's house and
south of the Hill. In order to get to Broadway, Tom would
have had to walk south through the woods or down a wooded path, for half a mile. To get to the spot near the beach at
the end of Broadway, where my pendulum kept pointing,
he would then have turned left and walked east for almost a

mile. He wouldn't walk down Broadway to the beach. My reading is incorrect, I thought. He'd be in a more protected place, closer to home. How I wished I had practiced more with the pendulum. Over and over I doused the map, and over and over I came up with the Broadway spot.

Then Nanda tried it. She didn't know the spot that my pendulum had chosen. Hers was different. A little down the beach from where mine was.

Out the door, still carrying Nanda's lovely earthy brew, I felt determined to tell Glenn what I had discovered, even though it felt all wrong. Back at the fire station, everyone was standing around looking toward the sky at a helicopter that hovered over a spot mid-island. Another helicopter hovered lower in the sky. For a half hour or more we gathered tidbits of information. "Glenn," I said, "if this turns out not be the spot, I have another place we could try, o.k.?"

"O.K.," he said, though he must have known by then that Tom had been found.

While I was with Nanda, Cynthia had left our team of searchers on the beach and intuitively run up to the woods beyond the Hill, where she and others, coached by those in the helicopter, found Tom alive.

Some members of the community stayed on to talk and eat. Others, like me, drifted away. I needed to be alone, to allow the melancholy to wash over me and to think about *what it means to search.* Suddenly, too, I remembered that my bread dough was still sitting in the bowl on my kitchen counter.

Tom was transported by boat to a nearby hospital where he was held and cared for by his family before he passed away.

— what it means to search —

After I wrote the personal narrative "Search," I discovered some details surrounding Tom's disappearance, some details that I decided to incorporate into a fictionalized story about Lone.

Lone

Lone stepped, one wobbly leg at a time, through the doorway to the outside of the red cedar shingled cottage he and Ayla had owned for all the fifty years of their island life together. He turned to face the door and lifted one skinny arm, finger outstretched from the knobby hand, long before it was needed to touch the button, which he squinted to see in the waning light of a January afternoon. The lock clicked with a finality that stunned him a little bit. He pulled his thin beige sweater around him, unbuttoned.

In his addled mind, Lone was always searching for the way "home." Ayla, a former nurse at the Veterans' Hospital, understood the confusion in Lone's mind, and her life focused on love and protection for him. The tug of war between the home- seeking man and the woman protector had created more tension lately. Just a week ago, Lone arose in the middle of the night to escape protection, and Ayla had given in to neighbors' willingness to keep an eye out for him, to wrap him in a blanket and call if he showed up in the middle of the night in their basement, naked.

The sun slipped behind the Hill. Til drifted like gauze behind a hawthorn in the near distance, and she silently watched. That January afternoon she might have alerted Lone's wife who was baking bread with a friend at the north end of the island, gone for only an hour, gone with Lone in the house watching TV. "I'll be back soon, Hon," she had said. "I'm going to Margie's." Til might have tapped a branch at Margie's window, shaking the energy in the cozy island kitchen so that her friend would sense with a familiar urgency known to all caretakers of elderly loved ones, trying to slide quietly out the door, might have shaken the energy so that Ayla would have bolted out of that kitchen and driven home immediately to find Lone walking down the dirt path leading away from their home. The island spirit woman might have done that. But she did not.

After fifteen years of decline into the abyss of forgetfulness and disorientation precipitated by the plaque that clouded his brain, Lone, at eighty-three years old, was at the end of his time on earth. Til knew that. She herself had been a guiding spirit for those in pain for as long as stories have been told on the island.

Til had kept watch over Lone, closely for the past few months since his bout with pneumonia, since his labored breathing starved his poor brain of oxygen, especially since last week when he wandered out of the house in the middle of the night. She waited for the time that she could help him depart, to go home, in peace and dignity.

After a moment's hesitation to consider the final click of the lock, Lone turned with his back to the door and shuffled away. Lone, slight of body, weighing only a hundred pounds now, moved, except for the shuffling sound, silently along the dirt path, leading west to the center of the island. Somehow it didn't matter that the sun had set and that he was entering the shadows of the two hundred acre woodland. It didn't matter because Til was singing, and he followed her song, stumbling only now and then over an exposed root *along the well-worn deer path.*

Fifty years ago Lone and Ayla had played as friends and lovers in those woods. They followed stonewalls just for fun, walked along the edges of streams looking for mushrooms, and reveled in the Indian paintbrush, its brilliant red flower, sharp against the dark floor and shadowed creek in the oak and maple forest. In one special place, they had found a clearing where they danced together. Time and again, they explored round and round the center of the island on the hill behind their home and ended their day at this clearing, where they danced as the sun set.

Now in the darkness Til sang and Lone followed.

In the meantime Ayla returned home to find Lone gone. She called one friend and then another. People gathered, friends and neighbors who would search for him. Eventually, island fire and rescue vehicles raced to her home and then to a grassy widening in the dirt path, where Lone had just walked into the woods.

— along a well-worn deer path —
Some simply escape to freedom for a while.

An Encounter

Field glasses in hand
I headed north
Along the path
To catch the osprey
On the nest or in flight.

Mist fed all plants green,
Wild greens of every shade, and
Dampened my jacket.
I lowered my head and
Caught the stampede of footprints
Cast in softened soil.

What is the story here?
Hoof prints too small to be a horse,
Too large for a deer.
Scuffled, like a hurried meeting
And an escape.

A mile along the path
I lifted my eyes from the story
Written there.
Like pastoral guards,
Three cows stood in the path.
They posed, looking softly at me.
Where was my camera?

While the calf nursed, the bull
Took his place behind the cows
Just to be there, large, imposing.

For a while I stood.
What about the ospreys?
I wanted *to see them* on the nest.

The bovine beasts stood their ground.
I could have walked into the crowd,
Interrupted them, tested them.
What would they do? These huge
Creatures with gentle eyes.
Would the bull stomp?
Would the mother charge to protect her calf?
They seemed content there in the path,
Free for the moment from their pasture.

For a minute or two
We looked at each other.
Then, I turned back,
Filled with thoughts of the meaning of encounters
With strangers
And what it means
To walk away.

—to see them—

As I wrote this short personal narrative, it seemed to me that the fox had a perfectly free life here on Harmony Island. Since the writing, however, the foxes have all but disappeared.

Fox Kit

Early one morning with the intention of viewing the ospreys at their nesting site near the crossroads, I turned off the dirt road onto a path near the marsh. My mind was on the ospreys, so I was startled to see a furry ball about twenty feet in front of me in the middle of the path.

Two fox kits had been born in late March or early April. A number of times during my daily walk I had seen them romping down the road further northwest, and once, in the driveway of a summer resident, I saw what may have been the mother. Sick and scraggly looking, she had paused, then walked to the south side of their yard, *stood there, and watched me.*

Now a single fox kit lay on that same grassy path near the osprey nest. Not wanting to disturb the kit's morning slumber, I approached quietly, then turned and walked back out to the gravel road, and continued on toward the beach. Along the way I listened to the birds and noted the flowering crab apples planted by the Trail Gang, volunteers who cut and mow walking paths through our woods and who plant trees for our community.

An hour later on my way back home, I walked down the path again to see if it were clear. The sun was a little higher in the sky. Now it shone directly on the kit still lying there. For a moment I thought it might be dead, so

I inched a little closer. Then the sun caught a twitch of an ear.

I smiled and returned to the road, leaving the little one contented in the patch of sun.

—stood there, and watched me —

Maybe the reason the fox have disappeared is that we do have coyotes now. Or, maybe the disappearance of the fox has nothing whatsoever to do with the coyote.

Coyote

Two weeks ago toward mid-afternoon I turned right out of my driveway and walked northwest along the path that I enjoy so much for its uncluttered feeling, its clean stretch of gravel road. Low golden switch grass, bull briars and taller cedars flanked each side of the path. A quarter mile along the way another gravel road veers off to the right and my road continues into a hollow where smells linger, especially the musky scent of deer.

Just before that junction a small to medium dog-sized critter, walked toward me. I was amused, as I am when I meet a deer on one of my walks. Habitually, I continue walking as the deer walks toward me and wait for the moment when the deer realizes that I am not another deer.

This was not a deer, but I felt the same amusement. Perhaps a hundred yards away, the critter noticed me, paused to look, then walked off to the left and into the brush. The animal literally disappeared as it was perfectly camouflaged.

At the end of road, I turned left and headed toward the beach road. There ahead of me was the same animal, walking along the road as I was. It had cut through the brush at the corner and popped out onto the road. Even without my glasses on, I could tell that this was clearly not a fox. It was a bit taller than a fox, the coloring was different, all grays light and dark as opposed to the foxy reddish color.

The tail was not that extraordinarily long tail that the fox carries, straight out behind as it scoots along. No, this tail was fuzzy, but shorter, and it hung down rather than straight out. The color of the tail was dark and light gray.

The most distinctive difference between the animals — fox and coyote —was the style of the walk. What I now believed to be a coyote literally bounced along with a light-footed rhythm.

My mammal books did not help me and I could not speak with anyone on the island about the sighting. One friend would take a protective stance toward children and family. He would threaten to shoot it. Another would be distressed that the deer, a great joy in his life, would be endangered.

Maybe I could ask a neighbor toward the south end of the island, the only person who has dared to talk with me about "her" coyote, the one that visited her for years before it was shot on the island and identified by the Department of Environmental Management as a coyote.

At first, I hoped my critter was a coyote, another animal to be part of our community. Then I wondered what chance a coyote would have with the stories that circulate about them? Humans here and elsewhere fear — and therefore want to *destroy*— *the unfamiliar*, what falls outside our normal living patterns or sense of personal safety. Maybe coyotes attack babies! They attack cats and small dogs! Who knows what else might be attributed to this shy but able predator who might help to keep our deer population in check, naturally.

— destroy — the unfamiliar —

How hard it is to live with critters that threaten perfect control over our gardens and our lives! If truth be told, one day we can have a generous philosophy about garden marauders as described in this personal narrative; but after a serious raid, we just might pull out the traps.

Breathing Holes

Allison called yesterday looking for a copy of *Where Storms are Beautiful*. Save the Bay is opening its new center and she thought it might be nice to have a copy there. I had only six copies left. We talked for a while, then she agreed to loan her copy. At a later time maybe I could present a new copy to them. "Ah, that's good," I said. "Thank you."

I hung up the phone and knew that today is the day to begin *Where Storms are Still Beautiful* (which eventually became *Tossed and Shaped by the Distant Sea*). The northeast wind howls on this our second day of a nor'easter. Matt took the dory out of the water yesterday in anticipation of the storm. Our Sea Hawk is sitting in Bristol without an engine, waiting for a new one to be installed.

So, almost twenty years after the writing of *Where Storms are Beautiful,* we are still here. We're still here gardening, participating in the community, tending our fire, and repairing what breaks. What's new is that we are on a construction crew, building a house on the mainland with our son, Matt's son. What's new is that I am writing fiction. What's new is that I am studying medicinal plants now — with my daughter Laurie — doing advanced studies in East

Barre, Vermont, with Rosemary Gladstar and other top tier herbalists at the Sage Mountain Herbal Retreat Center.

What's new is that I see the world differently at 65 than I did at 47 when I wrote the first *Storms*. I see the world more clearly now, as it truly is and as it has always been, as a living, breathing entity.

This morning Matt and I discussed the vole holes in the back near the compost bin. Voles are mouse-sized rodents that live in tunnels deep in the ground and that feed on roots, especially those luscious roots of carrots and sweet potatoes in gardens like ours. We had thought of dropping a mineral oil combination down the holes to send them elsewhere. But as I flushed the toilet, then washed up at the sink and brushed my teeth, I thought of how much water goes into the ground. How could the ground absorb so much, I wondered. Then, I thought of what I had read recently in a book called *The Lost Language of Plants,* written by one of our teachers, Stephen Harrod Buhner. He told of the Hopis saying that if the prairie dogs die there will be no rain. He quoted from a book telling of a government project to rid a section of Arizona of all the prairie dogs and how that project created an arid dead zone. Below that on the same page he tells of how earthworms and prairie dogs help the earth to respire. "As the moon passes overhead the underground aquifers rise and fall and Earth breathes out moisture-laden air. This exhalation of negative-ion-charged air through the many fissures and tubes opened by the bur-rowing creatures helps create rain "(60).

"What harm will the voles do as long as they are not in the garden?" I asked Matt. "Hey, and it's a way for the water to make its way into the air and dissipate." I smile. The holes remain.

As the wind howls and the rain slams against the northeast-facing window of my study, I know that in some ways nothing has changed here. The storms are still beautiful. In many ways, however, we are different. We have come to realize that *our lives are inextricably entwined* with the living, breathing earth.

— our lives are inextricably entwined —

This personal narrative is the story of my experience with ticks on Harmony Island. As an herbalist, I have read about the tick and about Lyme disease, but I do not pretend to be an expert. This is simply my story as an individual, my encounters with ticks one summer, and what I did.

To Live with the Tick

It is the first of July and I have already had eight embedded ticks, ones that needed tweezers to pull — without squeezing — from a tight hold on my skin. Over the past twenty-eight years that Matt and I have lived on the island, despite having had numerous tick bites, I have not yet had Lyme disease. This season is different, however. I have had the indicative flu-like symptoms — a couple of days of nausea, body aches, lethargy. They could be evidence of my body kicking out a minor threatening bug, or they could indicate infection with *Borrelia burgdorfei*, the Lyme spirochete.

Though this may sound perverse, I am glad, in a way, that I am dealing with the possibility of having Lyme disease. The experience will, at the very least, help my understanding of the process from thinking one has the disease through to the diagnosis and possible treatment.

Even on the island where the possibility of Lyme disease is a common factor in our lives, we react to it in very different ways. Some islanders keep a stash of antibiotics in the medicine cabinet. In the event of a tick bite, they immediately begin their own prescribed round of antibiotics. I don't want to do that. I feel uncomfortable with the overuse of antibiotics. Among other problems, they throw the whole immune system out of balance. Had I decided on that route, I would already have taken antibiotics eight times this summer and it is only the first of July!

After finding a tick, some folks go to the emergency room at the local hospital and ask for a Lyme test and a round of antibiotics to begin immediately. Our various reactions have to do with our own Lyme experience with family and friends, with fear of the disease, with an understanding of the strength or weakness of our own immune systems, and with the range of choices.

Our community has been ravaged by Lyme disease. For years the deer herd has been much too large for the limited land that we have on the small island where we live. Here the deer tick has a perfect opportunity to complete its tick–mouse–large mammal life cycle. Especially during and after a wet spring, ticks flourish.

Ticks! We have more than our share of them.

I ordinarily feel quite certain that I have found a tick within twenty-four to forty-eight hours of its being on my body. I feel the pinch of its existence, even during the middle of the night. I get up, go down to the bathroom, and fumble for the tweezers. I choose to live with the tick in an organic way. It is on my body. I pull it out. If the tick is found within forty-eight hours of its being attached, the risk of spirochetes having entered the body is close to nil.

Nobody is right or wrong in our individual responses to the threat of Lyme disease. We simply make different choices. I have made my choice. Now I do not feel well. Two weeks ago I saw my acupuncturist who recommended that I have a Lyme test. I called my doctor for a prescription for the test.

The medical system is difficult for seniors like me. Complications in the system delay diagnosis. It is necessary to have a "primary" doctor, just for the record. He is the one who is on the official list of primary care physicians and he would order the tests. Since I had seen this doctor six months ago for a musculo-skeletal issue, I thought I could call for a prescription for a Lyme test.

Not so. I had to see him. An appointment was scheduled.

Quick treatment of Lyme is necessary in order to wipe out the spirochete before it reproduces and becomes embedded in the body. A month after I initially thought I should have the test, I will see the doctor and I will be tested. When test results come in, perhaps my doctor will prescribe antibiotics. By then, if I have Lyme, it may have been in my body for two months. I feel angry and frustrated. On the island I have seen what happens when treatment is delayed, when Lyme becomes chronic and affects joints, heart, eyes, brain.

For a couple of days I mope around thinking this must be it. I have Lyme. Then, I begin to think as one trained in the use of medicinal plants. My studies with Rosemary Gladstar have prepared me to think about healing and to take action. I remind myself that I know what to do.

During one round of my studies, Stephen Buhner, author of *Healing Lyme*, spent the weekend teaching at Rosemary Gladstar's Advanced Herbal Healing Course. With him was a beautiful tall and slender young woman from India, a woman who had carried Lyme disease in her body for five years. Buhner did an "intake" by asking questions and listening to her history. Of course, she had agreed to do this in front of our group so that we could see and hear the exchange and so that we could ask questions. We listened to his rationale for treatment as he suggested the steps she should take.

In his book Buhner offers a clear protocol for both prevention and treatment of Lyme disease. Powerful herbs block the path of spirochetes and boost the immune system to fight the disease. Others address symptoms, and thereby reduce discomfort. Medicinal plants can be used in conjunction with conventional treatment. Doctors use antibiotics. I reread sections of Buhner's book particularly the part about diagnosing — about how the testing often misses the diagnosis — and about treatment.

During his weekend at Sage Mountain, Buhner said that if you live in an area where a disease is endemic, a medicinal plant will grow there, a plant that will address that disease. He specifically named Japanese Knotweed. I did not know whether Japanese Knotweed grew on the island where we live, but I was eager to find out. After that weekend when I returned to the island, I found on my table a publication from the Research Reserve at the south end of the island. There in the center of page one was a photo of the invasive plant called Japanese Knotweed! I vowed to harvest that plant and process it.

Though I still had not harvested Japanese Knotweed, I started my treatment with the herb. It was in a homoeopathic dosage bottle, not what Buhner would like. He says to use the root of the plant. I also included two other herbs, Andrographis and Cat's Claw. Andrographis is antimicrobial, Knotweed is anti-inflammatory, and Cat's Claw improves immune function. Andrographis and Cat's Claw are in my herbal refrigerator, in capsule form, left over from my work on Lyme with my neighbors.

Six days later I saw my doctor. Until then I treated myself and thought about how to handle our meeting.

Buhner's book *Healing Lyme* gave me credence in insisting on getting the Western Blot (not the Elisa) test and on insisting that certain bands be reported, bands that would show possible early Lyme.

In the office I talked with my doctor about possible next steps, about other tests that are expensive but even more reliable than the Western Blot, and about successes and failures in diagnosing and treating Lyme. My doctor wrote the prescription for the Western Blot test and noted that certain bands be read.

By the time I received the results from my test, I was feeling better. The tests results were negative for Lyme disease.

The next time I think I have Lyme disease, I will call immediately for a test and, without delay, will begin my own treatment. The Japanese Knotweed that Matt and I harvested on the island is tinctured in an alcohol extraction and ready for use, and I still have Andrographis and Cat's Claw capsules in my herbal refrigerator. The tincture and the capsules made from *medicinal plants* can only benefit my body's immune system, as I continue to live with the tick.

Another book worth consulting is *Lyme Disease and Modern Chinese Medicine, by Dr. Qingcai Zhang and Yale Zhang. Check out lymeinfo.net, too.*

— medicinal plants —

When I entered the study of medicinal plants, my life changed. While I always felt connected to the natural world — to the animals and plants with whom I share my life — this study added a whole new dimension to our relationship.

She Talks to Flowers

She talks to flowers.
Who does?
Grace.
Do you think she's lost it, then?
No.
What then?
She's changed, still solid as the eroding rock at the water's edge but now quivering with vibrations of plants.
Will she last here among us?
I don't know. Maybe.
She'll have to grow her hair long, weave it into a braid, and wear a kimono, high necked, loose fitting, down to her knees or ankles, white. As a signal. A flag of surrender.
We'll need to walk more softly around her and *touch her with gentleness.*

—touch her with gentleness —

Again I write about community and our lives here, not in an idealized way, but simply the way it is.

Communities overlapping

Ann is still wearing black, still mourning her mother's passing, though she's quiet about that. We sit on the bench outside Marcy's store and we talk about the island's one-room schoolhouse, about the possibility of its closing and about the work the community has done to create alternatives for the school committee and the town council. Her husband Bob has been the chief negotiator. Probably twenty other islanders have attended meetings on the island and on the mainland, and they have made calls and written letters. Pat Rossi, another neighbor, has been the coordinator for our save-the-school activities, figuring out rides across the bay for those going to evening meetings, posting dates of meetings here and there, keeping track.

Ours is a historic K-5 one-room schoolhouse. This year four children attend classes here. The prospect is that next year we may have two students. Yet only a few years ago we had thirteen. New houses are being built and many others are for sale. Next year we could have not two but ten.

The 10:30 ferry has come and gone. Ann and I still sit. Alone now. Marcy comes out of the store with her broom. "O.K., lift your feet," she says. Ann and I exaggerate the lifting of our feet as Marcy pushes the broom under them, taking dried mud with it. The day is murky, but there's a break in the rain that has deluged the island for the past month.

"It's worse down there," Ann points to clumps of mud at the top of the stairs.

"Hey, Marcy, how long do we have to keep our legs up?" I say. We laugh together. Ann and I continue our conversation, moving from the school to politics in the town, taxes, and other issues that concern members of a community.

I peek into the store and see that it's 11:00 a.m. "I've gotta go," I say. "Lots to do at home before the writers arrive."

Tomorrow, my friends — who have been sharing their writings for over ten years — come for a retreat, our ritual early summer reunion and work session. One *community* overlaps another — the island trying to preserve our school and a quality of life for our families and teacher writers who call themselves Educators Writing for Change.

— community —

We remember John and our music with him. To keep him alive, we replay music and moments over and over.

Remembering John and Music at the Church

Friday

Ten minutes early for our rehearsal at the church, John is already standing near the big gnarled trees near his house with his two black cases, one for his mandolin, one for the guitar. In the car we head for the church, about five minutes away, behind and south of the community hall.

John is agitated, as he always is before a performance. Matt, Allison, and Cynthia will not be with us for rehearsal for our playing music at mass on Sunday. Matt is working on a roof with Mattie; Allison and Cynthia had obligations on the mainland.

Glenn, Malcolm, John, and I set up folding chairs off to the side of the podium and the altar, in the brown-shingled island church. During the rehearsal, we stumble along. Most important for John is his latest creation, "Waltz of the Angels." We botch the beginning, but manage fairly well through the rest of the song, even though I still do not know how to play the harmonica part. We feel good about "One Day at a Time" because we have at long last kept good timing. John has difficulty with "A Closer Walk with Thee," a hymn he is playing alone. He lashes out because one of us hits a guitar string as he plays.

Saturday

On my way home from the post office, I stop at Malcolm and Cynthia's so we can talk about John, how to respect him, as a composer of music and a life-long musician, as an elderly man. We talk about how to help him to hold on to some power in the group, without his usurping it from the group. He wants me to sing "One Day at a Time" alone, but "It's a group song," I tell him. Would they mind, I ask, if I just started the song alone, four lines, then we could all join in. They smile and we know that it isn't a problem. We'll do what we have to do to make good music and to keep our John content.

Sunday

On the way to church we pick up Allison, dressed in her funky leg tights and shortish skirt, red water shoes and straw hat, and we pick up John's instruments. He has driven to the ferry to get his sister and her friends. Malcolm, Cynthia, and Glenn arrive on time. Cynthia is dressed in black and white, black shoes, hose, dressed "properly" for church, as my father would have said. I'm in linen pants, a Guatemalan loose-fitting embroidered blouse and moccasins. Matt and Malcolm and Glenn wear shorts or summer pants. And John. At eighty-five years old, John wears his Department of Environmental Management uniform, tan shirt with insignia, tan shorts, with a belt showing that he's lost weight since he purchased the uniform. But dress is not what we're about. It's the music that matters.

We tune up during the half hour before participants arrive. "Waltz of the Angels," means a lot to John. He says he created the song when he was recovering at his son's house from an accident. At the T-wharf, his truck had lurched forward, flown off the dock, and landed in fifteen feet of water. During recovery, in his room was a statue of an angel holding a mandolin. She was his inspiration.

A section of the "Waltz" is elusive to me. I just can't get it on the harmonica. While the guitars have to play softly (at John's insistence) during most of the waltz (after all there are four of us on guitar), I ask them to play a little louder during the harmonica part, to smooth any ragged edges on my playing.

Before mass begins, we play "Waltz of the Angels," better than we have done it before, ever. Ah, this is a good way to begin.

Our second and last song for the group is "One Day at a Time." We love this song, but we have problems with it, especially in the timing. I try to move my body in time so that we can all keep to that beat, Matt on the bass keeps a steady beat for us, too, but somehow, especially during the instrumental interlude, we break apart and cannot find our bearings. We continue with the vocal. The song is hard to sing in the morning. It is high, at the very top of my range. I close my eyes to remain focused and we play it well.

Later as we review our performance, we agree that the timing was off again on "One Day at a Time." Still, the audience loved it, as they did John's "Waltz of the Angels."

Monday

At 6:30 Monday morning John calls to talk about how we played yesterday, how great the harmonica sounded, how he screwed up, how people cried when we played and sang "One Day at a Time." He is happy.

— We remember —

For islanders whose family has been here for generations, both place and family draw them back. But when a couple is new, like us, having lived here just over a quarter of a century, a family's coming to the island is more duty than need.

Family and Roots

At 7:00 this morning a pair of sparrows huddled on a single fence post four feet away from their home. Nesting material, soft cottony stuff and straw, hung out of the birdhouse as though a robber had come through, ransacked the place and left. I felt sad.

Fourth of July is a family time here on the island. Waves of folks pour off the ferry in anticipation of this day of celebration. They are families coming back to the nest. No evidence exists of ransacking, only flags, coolers, children skipping along. It is a sad time for me.

I have a loving family, but we are not a tribe, like Matt's family. Nor do we have roots here on the island, like Matt's family and the Homans', Cathy and Dick, Sharon and Dave. Last night on the fourth, Sharon and Dave invited us to their house. They were having Sharon's cousins over for veggies and snacks. Sharon wanted them to spend a little time with her elderly father and to show their new house in progress, too.

At Sharon and Dave's we sat around with folks who could trace their roots on the island to the Civil War! Last week we had talked with someone who said to us that we must certainly now "belong" to the island. After all we have been here for twenty-six years. "Oh, no," I said.

"We'll always be newcomers." Matt's family vacationed here for a couple of weeks in the summer from 1940 to 1954. We moved here full time in 1980, but the folks who really belong are those whose family histories intertwine and reach back. Sharon's family has been here for more than a hundred years. Their roots are deep.

Fourth of July is a sad time for me only in that I yearn for my family to be here with me, not necessarily on this particular day, but for some day or days during the summer. The garden is lush, like a paradise, the greens and textures tease an artist to take up the palette. Birds twitter and chirrup and wail in our beautiful silence. The twittering of the two on the fence post this morning touched me as I made breakfast in my kitchen. This is what so many people yearn for and we have it to share.

How lovely that we have friends from all over who come to the island, that we have neighbors who are as appreciative as we are, who revel in the island. Our lives are full and good. When we've been *away* or when we come home through a storm, we feel lucky to come back to our own nest.

No one has come through to rob us or disrupt our homestead. Home is sweet. We are whole and spiritually fulfilled. But the longing is deep for my loving family that has no roots here, no reason to come except to see Matt and me.

— *away* —

When my granddaughters were nine and thirteen years old, my son Lee invited me to go to Paris with him, his wife Joël, and the two girls, Sarah and Caroline. I spoke a little French. We stayed about a mile apart. Each day I met them for our daily adventures. "The Look" is a personal narrative and part of that adventure.

The Look

A light mist fell that gray morning when I stepped out of my Paris hotel in the shadow of Invalides. I was determined to walk to the Louvre to meet my son and his family. Though I did not know exactly how far it was, I relished following the twists and turns of the map and had ample time for taking a wrong turn and doubling back. I wanted to feel Paris — in the air, in my pores, under my feet.

I hesitated on the single step to the sidewalk. Umbrella raised high, a stalky-legged woman in spike heels and a vibrant red coat clicked past two miniature yellow cars parked along the road. For a moment the woman seemed ten feet tall. I considered the mist, the woman with the umbrella, and my own ankle length raincoat, inside which I felt secure, though I had only used it to protect myself from short bursts of rain at home as I dashed from the car to my place of business. I loved to feel the mist on my hair, knew it was better than any curling device that others might use for theirs, loved to feel unencumbered and unrestrained by hat or hood. In my pocket I fingered the folded map and stepped down to the sidewalk. I looked right toward a sidewalk café, breathed in the Paris morning, and turned left.

Up Duquesne to the corner and on toward Invalides,
I walked. Then the rain came. In khaki trench coats, tan
or black raincoats, everyone rushed along, now. All other
pedestrians had umbrellas. Two men stood under a rolled
up awning in a doorway. Sidewalks were narrow. Umbrellas clicked as they were raised or lowered to accommodate
those passing in the other direction. Everyone squeezed
toward a building as a car splashed along sending spray up
from the road. Heavy drips fell to the middle of the sidewalk from overhanging roofs five or ten stories up. It took
all of my concentration just to maneuver and progress along
my way.

Women hustling here and there never looked at me —
or perhaps at anyone else. The men did. Though I would
not be considered a beautiful woman, on this day I felt
beautiful. Why did the men look at me and the women did
not? Do the men look at every woman? I wondered.

I am small. On this day it did not occur to me that
I had passed the half-century mark and was closing in on
sixty. My nose is slightly beaky and in photos I have always
avoided a profile shot. I am vital and rosy cheeked. When
I smile, my eyes light up. Had my hair not been silver gray,
I might have passed for fifteen years younger than my age.
Certainly, though I hardly ever considered age, I felt young,
or perhaps ageless, though I had never said that to anyone.
Certainly I had not considered my own appearance, that is,
to attract the looks of men or anyone else, for that matter.
For me this trip to Paris felt more of an inner journey.

Because of business, my son and his family had the
rare opportunity to spend time in Paris. Since he might be
spending a good deal of his time with his business at hand,
he invited me to come along. I spoke passable French and
I could be a companion to his wife and children.

I loved Paris. My first time there had been as a gift to myself and my first husband after I graduated from college and had worked for a year. Before we became accustomed to my working full time, the new salary had seemed extra. So I insisted we take a European trip and that we visit Paris.

Other times over the years, I had traveled with this man or that, a friend, my second husband. Paris was special to me, one of the most romantic cities in my experience. Each of my companions had come along to please me. Although I felt the same in many ways as I had when I first saw Paris, I knew that in the interim thirty years I had changed. I had been through the joys and pain of relationships, of life, surviving the anguish of divorce, growing accustomed to living as a single parent with adolescent children, moving close to death and surviving, then remarrying and living a life on Harmony Island with my husband now of many years.

This was my first trip to Paris without a travel mate. Though my son and his family would meet me for each mid-day's adventures, the mornings and evenings were mine. My hotel was a mile from theirs, so I felt like an independent traveler.

By the time I approached the gold-domed Invalides and the huge Musée de l'Armée, a driving rain had seeped through my raincoat. My hair was plastered to my head, and I felt almost ridiculous being the only one on the rushing sidewalks without an umbrella.

Around the corner and across the street from the Musée de l'Armée, the red awnings of a café triggered a deep breath. A smile rose up from the deep appreciation of this luxurious sight and a smile spread over my face as I entered what felt like a retreat.

Just inside the door I peeled off my raincoat, and adjusted to the wetness that had seeped through my suit coat and my turtleneck. Water dripped from the coat as I looked for a chair or a hook from which to drape it.

Most of the tiny round tables in the café were arranged along the perimeter of the walls. At each, men in black suits sat, half leaning in toward each other in conversation, half looking toward me, as I stood at the door. At first I thought this might be a men's club, then at the far end of the room, I saw an Asian woman and five Asian men, deep in conversation. Only one table was empty, the one in the middle of the floor. Knowing that I would be on display there in all my wetness, I moved without hesitation to the table. I draped my coat over one chair, then slid around to the other, so that my back was to a wall without windows, and I faced the center of the room.

At my right was a bar for the preparation of coffee. Three tables of men seemed squeezed up against the coffee bar. Windows swept around from slightly behind my left arm, to the corner near the door, which was ahead of me and slightly to the left. I could see into the far end of the room, almost a separate little room, where the Asians sat. They were still immersed in conversation. All other eyes in the room rested on me. About twenty men and a woman sipped coffee.

I kept my eyes lowered, but enjoyed being observed, their eyes on my, their looks of approval, though I knew I must look like a drowned rat. Suddenly I was aware of how women know these things and how they learn to signal. I did not smile, rather I kept a peaceful look, and when one man clearly looked directly at me, though I saw the look, I did not meet it. I was, after all, a happy woman, in a marriage of more than twenty years, and I was, after all, almost sixty years old.

The aroma from the tiny cup of espresso set before me nearly sent me into tremors, so magnificent an experience was it. I sipped at the spoon and restrained myself from inhaling the entire cup of coffee in one gulp. I would make it last as long as possible, and drink in the experience.

There, sitting with my espresso in the middle of the café, I flicked back to an earlier experience in the Charles de Gaulle airport where passengers enter Paris. There at the airport travelers had stood in a long customs line. My line had not moved at all. Eventually, the entire line shifted to a new spot. The new window closed, and the line moved again. No one had grumbled. Each individual simply stood and waited.

Out of the corner of my eye I had seen an older man, sixty-five or so, dressed in a cashmere coat, reeking of success. I watched him walk toward me. This man pretended not to see me, as he stepped right into the spot in front of me. I stood off to the side a bit and glared at him. Boldly, calmly, I looked right at this face. As if my eyes were magnets to his, he turned to look at me.

"Do you know me?" he had asked in heavily accented English.

"No, I don't think so," I said calmly, and he moved to another place further back in the line.

In the café, I thought about the power of a look as I donned my wet coat and walked again into the driving rain.

Whenever I felt insecure about my way, I stepped under a rolled up awning and took out the sodden map, tearing now at the folds. Through steaming glasses, I checked road signs, refolded the map and moved on. Sometimes my glasses were so steamy I could not see the map. I searched for a dry tissue or piece of fabric from my clothing to wipe them. There was nothing. Tall buildings lined the narrow streets. No charcuterie, patisserie, or other shop offered shelter. I walked down one street and came to another that I recognized. Eventually, despite the starts and stops, the doubling back, I arrived, thoroughly drenched, at the arch of the Louvre, where I was to meet my son. I was a half hour early.

A cold wind blew through the arch and I searched for a dry niche, a niche out of the wind, from which I could see my son and his family and where they could see me.

The looks continued. Men pulled up in cars, waited for the light to change, and looked. Young men on bicycles and walkers looked.

I watched a handsome European walk past me. His black coat reached to mid calf. The cut emphasized his wide shoulders and narrow hips. Cleanly cut wavy hair reached to just above the collar. In another age and another time I would think, "How romantic!" I would make a decision about meeting the look or lowering my eyes.

The sharp wind swept through the tunnel of the arch. A bus stopped at the light across the street. A half dozen tourists stepped onto the sidewalk, and received a splash from a car moving past the front of the bus. I stood straight, shoulders back. Inside myself, however, was a little person huddling against the cold, creeping now along the skin of my arms.

"Now," I thought, "It's all the same." In conversation with myself, I asked, "What?" And I answered, "The man, the image, the smell, the look — the romantic notion. The look of each man is the same. While the looks are a matter of curiosity to me, they have no bearing on my life, except to attest to the fact that I exist."

"Eventually," my husband had said during one of their dinnertime conversations, "you live together and it's different." Maybe he meant that the romance was gone, but I hadn't taken it that way. I had thought he meant that when you begin to know someone, the look is different. The quivering is gone.

If that is what he meant, I thought maybe he was right. Something happens when you live with a person. He is no longer a wonder in the sense that a stranger is. You still notice how and when he looks, and when he doesn't. And maybe the look becomes something deeper, a look into each other's day, into worries and concerns, into the soul and what it means to live together in an ongoing human relationship. The reaffirmation of ageless beauty becomes a mutual daily ritual.

"Hey, Mom." My musings were interrupted as my son looked at me and waved from the pyramid in front of the Louvre. I carefully crossed the street and entered another world.

— *watched* —

This poem was written for *my daughter*, Laurie.

Your Watching Tree

Outside the window stands your watching tree.
Each day when the sun bathes your room in light, you
Sit on your bed, cross-legged, a child, to see
A world through a spider's web, covered with dew —

A sleek black crow, a wren, a mourning dove,
Capped catbirds, sparrows, and the regal jay.
A possum sleeps. Is he dead in the tree above?
The wind shakes the tree and the dead one skitters away.

Darkness falls and black air quivers. A mink breaks
Into the coop and spatters the inside red
With the blood of chicks. Is it their screaming that wakes
Us in the night? Two roosters alive; four hens dead.

Within you the critters, their lives and deaths, still live
And from this source you thrive and reach out to give.

— my daughter —

In sickness and in health, we belong to and depend upon our communities.

In Sickness and in Health

My daughter calls from a hospital in Amsterdam, upstate New York, a half hour from her home. Normally a robust, energetic woman, she says in a shockingly weak voice that she and her husband picked up a virus or bacterial infection. She is dehydrated and ill.

"I can't-believe how many people I know here," she says softly into the phone. "The girl inserting my IV was a former student. She worried that she wouldn't do it right. I laughed and told her she wasn't going to get a grade on this," she says. "Another nurse came by and said she thought my name sounded familiar. She's going to be in my class in the fall."

Community. Hers is a spread out, rural community, quite different from our compact community on the island where we live. Like many of us, Laurie and her husband Jim are members of a number of communities, among them one that she has created as a teacher at the community college and another that she and her husband have created around their own lifestyle and homesteading.

Matt and I have an extended community because we were teachers in the same mainland town for many years. So often now those who service our cars or who work in testing labs are former students. We went to a wedding not too long ago and I met a former student there. He had been in my seventh grade English class twenty-five years ago. At that time, we had the dreadful task of teaching students parts of speech during the first six weeks of seventh grade. To make the learning of prepositions a bit fun, I taught the preposition song. First the boys sang, then the girls, then they all sang together. I told them to sing in the shower at home. If they sang, I said, they'd *never forget* their prepositions. There at the wedding, my former student sang for me: "About, above, across, after, against, among around... " to the tune of "Battle Hymn of the Republic." We laughed together.

As Laurie talks with me about being surrounded and cared for by people she knows, I reflect upon our various communities — our family, our former students and teaching colleagues, our island friends and neighbors. I remember, too, my own pain and rescue by members of my community. It was an experience so special that I fill with tears and have trouble finding words to express it.

My daughter is well cared for, I think. She knows it and feels comforted.

A few days later, however, Laurie and I talk. She is home, but not feeling better, in fact, feeling worse. And so, I have the melancholy pleasure of going to New York to take care of my friend, my herbal companion, my daughter, and member of my most primal and beloved community.

—*never forget* —

Oops! We were so busy, we forgot to check the dates!

Movie Night

These days it is hard to know whether I am early or late or on time for anything. We are still building young Matt and Rachel's house on the mainland. *Planning is difficult* with our continuing schedule, ever in flux. One more week and we will be able to plan again. They will be back in school. Construction will slow to weekends, though we will still work hard — along with the rest of the family — as they are hoping to be in the house by October.

I had not opened my e-mail in two weeks! When I did, the first thing I noticed was that a movie would be playing down at the south end. This is a fairly new, lovely occurrence on the island, thanks to Bob Marshall and Pat Richards. Once a month we have a movie and potluck dinner. On e-mail I saw that the movie would be "Million Dollar Baby" which Matt and I had wanted to see last year when we were in Jackson Hole. I urged Matt to try on Friday to get home from Mattie's so we could see the movie. I would be staying home to catch up. "No problem," he said. He wanted to see it, too.

On Friday I made a lovely gazpacho soup, time consuming, especially since I was also making mustard pickles. I wanted to make it for Cathy Homan, who loves the gazpacho, as well as for the potluck meal. Matt called Sharon and Dave to talk about the movie. Did they want to join us? That morning I also started bread to take with the soup for the potluck.

About nine o'clock, Pat Richards called. She never calls me, so I knew something unusual was up. "Grace," she said. I tried to catch the tone of her voice. "Ah, about the movie. Sharon told me this morning at the boat that Matt had called and that you guys were planning to go to the movie tonight," she hesitated. "But the movie was two weeks ago."

So that's the way our summer has been. I laughed uproariously with Pat. She said we'd missed a good movie. "I love gazpacho," she said. "Maybe you can bring me some."

—Planning is difficult —

Jan and I have been friends since high school, so we can challenge, chide, support, and love each other as though we were family. This piece is a reflection on the words of my friend.

Your Choice, Grace

Last Friday I had lunch with an old friend. "How are you?" she asked, not just to ask, but because we are old friends. We always want to know REALLY, how are you?

"I'm just fine," I said, knowing how lucky I am to have good health and a happy life. "There is one thing, though, and that is TIME. I'm struggling with time," I said.

My friend lives off the island. She leads a mainland life, meaning that her car is outside her door and she can drive to the market, to yoga, to the doctor's. She has been laid up for the past seven months after an accident — and so has been tossed about in the turbulence of mind and body recovery. Until then, however, she seemed in control of her day. She could dash out to this meeting or that and be home in a couple of hours. As islanders we know that when we make a commitment to leave the island to attend a meeting, to meet a friend, or go to the doctor's, the day disappears like dust in the wind. Dashing out for an hour or two is not part of island culture. No markets interrupt our landscape. No doctor's offices sit on the dirt roads. The ferry runs in the morning and again late in the afternoon.

As we sat together over salad and tea, I tried to explain a little about my issues with choice and time management, but I gave up. I heard myself sound as though I were making excuses for not being on the mainland more often when

163

really a lifetime of journeying had brought me to a place,
unexplainable in an hour or two, a cultural and spiritual
place that I had not as yet articulated, to anyone.
We talked about other issues of concern to both of us, including the question: What does it mean to be on the far
side of sixty-five?

When we were ready to leave, she said, "It is your
choice to be that busy, Grace." I looked at her, knowing
there was so much more to say about choice — when we
make choices, how we make them, and what chooses us.

This morning, my husband Matt was digging a trench
behind the house, so I ate my breakfast quickly and dashed
upstairs to my desk in an attempt to write for an hour.
I have been working on the same chapter, the same ten
pages for several months. I get to my desk to write only an
hour, two at the most, each week.

After a quick read and a few copy editing notes on the
chapter, I opened my e-mail to find out what was happening with the island school closure issue. I knew this was my
morning to call the office of the Commissioner of Education
to schedule a hearing and to ask questions that friends and
neighbors had posed about the impending closure of our
K-5 elementary school.

The Hearing Officer's assistant could not assure me that
the date she had originally given would in fact be possible.
It had taken time and effort to get all seven of us on the
Island School Working Committee to agree on a date. The
ISWC had formed a year ago to explore ways to save our
one-room school. To set the original date for the hearing,
I had gone from house to house to talk with each mem-
ber. On the phone the assistant said, "I'll call the School

Committee's lawyer to see if he can make it then." My heart sank. Intuition informed me he would not be able to make that date. But the assistant was very accommodating, and she sent me over to a lawyer on the staff who could answer some of our questions. I glanced at the clock ticking off the day's time.

Our questions were scribbled on my pad. The lawyer seemed eager to answer all our questions, but when he referred me to this General Law and that one, to this web site and that one, my breathing sped up and eyes glazed over. I can't do this all day, I thought. So, I took the notes, with the intention of transcribing them into a clear list and sending them off to our committee. In an e-mail I would ask someone else to look into the laws. It was already one o'clock. Choices. Hmm.

I was in the midst of this work when someone yelled up from downstairs. "Grace, Grace." It was a neighbor from a couple of miles down the road. I saved what I had written and went downstairs. She was teary eyed, physically crumbling. As she hugged me and started to cry, I helped her into a chair. Miles away, her son is dying. Here on the island, her elderly mother approaches the end of her life. She wept, overwhelmed by facing death every day. I gave her some water, then the two of us sat at the kitchen table and I listened to her.

Matt came in from the transfer station, still filthy from digging his trench. He carried a monster of a rocking chair. "Do you want this?" he asked. "No," I said, both annoyed and amused at the interruption. He put it down in the living room, knowing I'd want to consider it later. He took his shower, then left for some errands on the mainland.

I stayed with my neighbor, offering her my ear. "Do you have time for this?" she asked.

"Yes," I said. And I did. It was a choice. I felt honored that she had chosen to sit with me at this turbulent time of her life.

Honored. When had I come to this? Years ago, who knows when, I might have considered such an interruption an annoyance. Perhaps a spiritual awakening seeps into our lives unnoticed, like the scent of sea salt or of the fragrance of cherry blossoms in springtime.

My neighbor and I spent time choosing flower essences, dousing with a pendulum to get the right ones for her, to help with calming. After working with the essences, she did seem much better. "A visiting nurse will be here tomorrow," she said. Every Wednesday a nurse from the Visiting Nurse Service comes to the island to tend to individuals who need help with home care and to run the monthly Blood Pressure Clinic here. My neighbor planned to ask what could be done to help her mother. The nurse would administer blood tests, too. As she was leaving, another neighbor pulled up, looking for a sander that his brother had loaned Matt. I called Matt and he talked with our friend, who found the sander in the garage.

Back upstairs, I blasted out an essay that has been requested of volunteers for the school, essays to become part of a packet of school information to substantiate our argument to keep the school open.

As I was finishing a draft of that essay, a call came from the Volunteer Nurse Services. "The VNS nurse who was supposed to come tomorrow will not be on the island," the caller said. "I thought you should know." For years, I have not been involved in the island Blood Pressure Clinics, nor have I had much contact with the VNS except for setting up the island Flu Clinics in the fall, but here I was now, chosen today as the contact person.

Maybe, this is a test of my spiritual progress, I thought. Am I ready to allow what comes to me, to come, ready to accept what is and to let go of what might be?

"O.K.," I said, "I'll try to find out about the clinic to cancel it, but it is VERY important that you call the family of my neighbor whose elderly mother needs advice. Please." I gave her the number of the neighbor who had just left me.

By now it was almost two o'clock. Straddling the chasm between being open to others on the one hand and having personal expectations on the other, I was still reaching for what might be. I wanted to plant seeds in the garden and wanted to walk on the beach. But I had to finish the work for the school. I blasted out an e-mail summary of my conversation with the lawyer at the Department of Education. Then I had lunch.

By three o'clock I was walking along the shore, feeling the wet low tide sand under my feet, inhaling sea scents. At that moment I knew I would not wish to change anything in my day, or, for that matter, in my life.

Back home, I had a telephone message from the Commissioner's office about possible dates for the hearing on the school closing. I went back on-line to send those dates to our committee, answered more e-mails, and sit here now writing at five o'clock.

So, yes, I have made choices. I live here on the island. Like most of my neighbors, I have become involved in the community. When I chose to live on island in 1980, I did not know that, many years later in retirement, my life would be taken up so much with community needs. I volunteer an hour every other week to teach writing at the island school, but during the past few years I have veered away from leadership roles on the island. I'm more of a respondent now. Hmm. I had never thought of that choice until this moment.

Choices. Yup. I've made them. And here I am. Busy and happy on a day like any other day. The details are different but the themes are the same. So what? I ask. Everyone is busy. That's the way life is. Maybe it doesn't matter so much what one does as how one does it. Perhaps orientation matters, too, and expectation. Is finishing the "to do" list all that important?

At six, I have knelt in the already lush garden to plant cauliflower and carrot seeds. The magic of planting has slowed me down, calmed me. I have chosen to take a shower and relax with a lovely dinner of chicken, brown rice and fresh rhubarb Swiss chard. Matt will be home much later.

Now, I am looking forward to revisiting the conversation with my old *friend* who said, "It's your choice, Grace." Still, I may need a few more years to learn how to articulate what is in my heart. Maybe the conversation needs to rest until we're seventy — or eighty — when I've had more time to think about making choices and what chooses us.

Or, maybe it is not about choice at all. Maybe it is simply about being.

— friend –

This short nonfiction piece is simply a light observation and questioning on the topic of couples, both bird and human.

Couples

Loud chirping draws me to the back door near the garden. There atop the birdhouse not two feet from the door are two little sparrows. One looks into the hole in the birdhouse, while the other stands on the roof and waits. Then the first steps aside and the second looks in. They flit to the birdhouse below the deck on the side of the house, the one where a pair of sparrows spent the summer. Again they take turns looking in and "talking."

They fly to the other side of the deck. One of the enormous birdhouses, made by our elderly friend John, hangs on the west facing side. They check that out then flit to another across on an east-facing pole under the Concord grape vine.

Why are they house hunting at the end of October? I wonder. And how is it that these two know equal power, each looking, each checking out the birdhouse?

As you enter Laurie and Jim's house in upstate New York, you walk through a greenhouse that runs the entire south-facing front of the house. The last time I was there I witnessed another birding activity that made me say, "Hmm." A female hummingbird had flown into the greenhouse and become trapped. She darted around wildly looking for a way out.

On the outside of the greenhouse appeared a male hummingbird. He flew to the far end of the greenhouse, exactly where the female was. Once he had her attention, he flew toward the open door, a few feet at a time. When he lost her to confusion, he flew back, regained her attention and eventually, patiently, led her to freedom.

Couples. *What is it that binds a pair* like the woodpeckers, the hummingbirds, Matt and me?

— What is it that binds a pair? —

Many historical threads are woven into "The Red Nun," a short story. When I was a child living in a beach community, for example, a neighbor's son hit a red nun channel marker with his small boat. He flew out of the boat and died. This incident has stayed with me for over fifty years.

The Red Nun

1945

The youngest of the three soldiers trotted into the Harmony Island Searchlight Army camp, breathless, "The *SS Black Point*! Sunk! Near the mouth of the Bay!" he said.

The May 5th attack created a screaming tension on and around the island, populated by one hundred fifty year round residents and three soldiers. Navy destroyers responded with depth charges that demolished the sub, while naval workers scrambled to stretch a submerged metal net across the shipping channel from the island's east shore to the west shore of the mainland, a mile away. For days the churning of chain clanged, clanged, clanged, as the chain netting was laid across the channel to protect bay waters and the capital city ten miles north of the island.

A week later, at the camp, high on the middle of the island's backbone, the jittery young soldier maneuvered the searchlight, scanning for threats from the air. He rattled on nonstop about what might be under the water, "Holy shit, one sub, maybe two, or a dozen frogmen — or whatever the hell Germans are called — crawling up out of the water!" The longer he saw nothing in the sky, the longer silence spread from sky to earth, the more certain he was that something was underneath, just beyond the Salem Point lighthouse.

Pete, the dark-eyed eldest soldier, paced. "Will you shut up, for Chris' sake," he said. The third soldier stared sullenly into the tiny flame under the coffee barrel.

The tense voices rattled the night as Andy whistled, then stepped from the darkness into the dim circle of frightened young men. Andy, "the kid," was an islander, a local, a sixteen-year-old kid, who had met the soldiers as they searched for snacks in his family's west side store. Andy often drank coffee and made a fourth for a card game with the three soldiers. This night he had brought his guitar along, thinking he'd get the guys to sing along, (They liked to sing) but the air crackled with tension and he set his guitar aside.

"Nothing's going through that net," Andy said. "It's safe." Though Andy was young, the soldiers listened to him. His being of the small island lent him some authority.

"Oh, yeah, Kid. If it's so safe, why don't you go swim in it? Swim across, for Chris' sake," said Pete.

Dark liquid in the barrel steamed over the low flame. The youngest soldier concluded his searchlight shift and stepped down from the platform. He dipped his cup into the barrel, hit grounds a couple of inches under the liquid, and then sat down with a half-filled cup. He jiggled his leg and set his hand down to calm it. Pete, who had barely sat down near the coffee barrel, stood up and resumed pacing, his dark eyes lowered. The kid both amused and irritated him.

That night Andy was jazzed, full of himself, and eager to lighten the mood. "O.K.," he said. "You guys think I'm just a kid, but, baby, I can swim. I've won every medal in

our swim club." The two year-round teenagers living on the
island traveled by boat every day to attend the town school
on the mainland, where Andy belonged to a swim club.
"I swim because I'm really a fish." Arms tight to his sides,
he wiggled fish-like to make them laugh. Pete wanted to
put a sock in his mouth.

Feeling the pressure of Pete's challenge, Andy said,
"O.K., Pete, I'll swim across the channel from here to the
mainland. I'll show you it's safe." But what did he know.
He was just a kid who thought that when you wanted
something to be safe, it was, that a matter of the will would
make it so. The sullen soldier who had just stepped up to
the searchlight remained expressionless, swinging the light
back and forth.

Pete stopped pacing. He stood, all six feet of his blocky
bulk, in front of Andy and whispered almost as though they
were part of a government conspiracy, "I'll up the ante."
He was twenty-two years old and always played for money.
Pete said, "Fifty bucks if you beat me to the other side."
Pete was crazier than Andy. Stirred by the tension of the
week's events, he was risking his army career. Andy hadn't
bargained for a race, but being sixteen, and thinking fifty
dollars was a mighty sum, he allowed himself a fleeting
glimpse of his parents asleep in their rooms behind the west
side store, then he said, "What do I have to lose? The bet's
on."

The searchlight soldier's mouth moved into a crooked
smile. "You're the one's gonna pay, Andy."

The jittery soldier said, "We can't be part of this. We'll
be up shit creek." He was excited by the whole venture,
but too scared to wish them good luck.

A sliver of a waning moon sliced the dark sky, and a
light chop kicked up on the bay waters from a southeast

breeze. Two figures appeared on the beach, like ghosts in the night fog, then they disappeared into the chilly dark water.

Like a hero about to be born and now a gaming fool, for the first few strokes underwater Andy really did feel like a fish. He popped up among shadows flashing in the chop and launched like a rocket into an Australian crawl that should take him across the shipping channel to the mainland. "Hell, it's only a mile, more or less," he had said. He swam full speed and didn't look back at Pete. True to his age, he knew if he gave it his best, he would win.

Andy had barely reached the red nun channel marker, when he thought he saw the periscope of a sub, barely fifty feet from him. "Pete! Pete! We're on top of a fuckin' sub!" He felt something, a boat hook, maybe, tugging at his leg, pulling him under.

Pete did not answer.

Close to the red nun, now, Andy gasped for breath. A voice from his childhood said, "Like fire or ice the nun could be a savior or a killer, depending how you handle her." It was the old one-armed captain, who had let Andy ride in the ferry wheelhouse with him. "She's there to signal boundaries. Respect that," he had said.

The red nun leaned toward him. He reached out, grabbed hold of her, and rode her up and down in the light chop. The nun's barnacles tore his cheek and his hands, and ripped his legs to shreds, but she let him hug her 'til he steadied himself. He looked around for Pete but he had disappeared. So had the periscope.

Andy swallowed down his sobs, pushed off from the nun, and swam back to shore. Giddy from the scare, in his soaked underwear hanging off his lanky frame, he galloped up the hill to the Army camp.

The youngest soldier screamed at the bloody vision and reached for his weapon. "You fuckin' forgot to whistle! I could' killed you," he said.

Andy tried to explain the fear that morphed out of the water and the hook that seemed to grab his leg. "It was the worst fuckin' nightmare of my life," he said. His cry turned to laughter. The other two joined him, partly from nerves. Andy could laugh at his own fears now that he was safe. Maybe they'd be safe, too. The young, jittery soldier handed him a wool blanket.

The serious soldier, still at the light, recovered from his laughter and said, "Where's Pete?"

"I never saw him. He's probably on the mainland by now," Andy said, teeth chattering. Wrapped in an army blanket, he slithered down the west side of the island, onto the porch of the store, through the barely squeaking door, and into his bed.

At 6:00 a.m. he bolted awake. "O m'god! How am I going to pay Pete $50?"

But Pete never appeared. Not that day. Nor the next. Nor any day after that.

"Get out of here, kid," said the serious soldier, when Andy went back to the camp to talk to them. "For your sake and ours, don't come back. O.K.?"

1985

As usual when the ferry was due at the Harmony Island dock, Jimmy Mahoney sat in his police car, surveying the scene. After two years on the job he knew the regulars, who came to pick up mail, to greet guests coming to the island on the ferry, or simply to socialize for the brief half hour, while friends and neighbors were coming and going.

He routinely saw Andy and Ruth who usually sat together on the bench. Jo Singleton, Laraine, and Louise, always met the 8:30, too. He saw who and what boarded the ferry for the mainland and who and what came off the ferry onto the island. Jimmy's job was to observe — and to help keep the island safe. His sharp eye caught a tall stranger with red hair, still on the ferry.

Keeping one eye on the red-haired stranger, coming off the ferry now, he observed Andy and Ruth whom he had known for only the two years since he and his young wife had moved to the island and he had become a policeman. Andy had lived on the west side of the island almost all his life. His parents and now he — because it had fallen to him after his parents died — ran the west side store. Jimmy figured him to be about sixty, give or take a year. He had heard Andy was a pretty crazy kid who would take a dare on a dime. His thick white hair standing straight up in the breeze, Andy now was known on the island as a kind and harmless senior citizen.

Ruth, the dark-haired beautiful Ruth, had lived on the island for much of her life. Ruth and Andy were buddies, good friends, almost like father and daughter. Like today, they often held hands as they sat on the bench waiting for the ferry. Once a week Jimmy watched as Ruth helped Andy roll an old wooden wagon onto the ferry to pick up supplies delivered from the mainland for his store. Together they loaded the wagon and rolled the thing off the ferry.

He saw her turn to Andy, but could not hear their conversation. They still held hands.

The two of them watched the tall red-haired stranger. A head above the others, he moved like crimson sea smoke on stormy waters. Everyone saw him, of course, — and no one knew him. He glanced at the watchers on the dock, then got into a sporty old convertible with a repaired ripped top, a used car rental, he'd sent over the day before to be parked by a ferry attendant.

Andy smiled, wanly. Jimmy knew his story. It seems everybody knew everyone else's story. By the time he was in his late twenties, both his parents had already died. With the exception of his high school years off the island and four years in the Navy, he worked the store as he still did today. When Ruth moved to the island as a teenager, she begged him to show her how to pluck a song on the guitar, the one he had learned on as a child. On the porch of the west side store, he taught her how to play. Now, as usual, he waited for groceries, quietly.

Ruth waited to help Andy with groceries and for what else? Jimmy wondered. It had been almost five years since she'd lost her husband Seth in a boating accident in a dense February fog. Before she began teaching at the island school, she and Seth used to commute in their boat to their mainland teaching jobs.

Jimmy watched Ruth and Andy sit quietly together. He saw Joe Singleton, his twisted body limping along; Laraine, with the wild frizzed hair, flirting with everyone, even Joe, — "Hi, Sweeties," she called out to Joe and Andy; — and Louise, who abruptly stopped at the bench to talk with Andy and Ruth.

"Good morning, Louise," Ruth said, distracted, as she stood up to move and came almost chest to chest with the other woman.

Andy nodded to Louise, then to Ruth said, "You ready?" Together they rolled his wagon, squeaking and groaning, onto the ferry to collect the groceries.

At low tide Sunday morning at sunrise, while Andy was still asleep in the back room of his west side store, Ruth walked White Sand Beach on the northwest side of the island. The beach swept in a grand arc that curved again at its southernmost edge and rose to a lofty hill at the northern tip. For purists who liked to think of the island as a grand fish — the head at the north end and the tail south — this was the glitch. From the air it appeared as though a larger fish had taken two bites out of the fish's belly, an unsettling thought, if such comparisons mean anything.

Flat calm, grays and blues shimmered, like veiled sweeping searchlights, in the indirect cast of the morning sun. Ruth usually walked a marching step, long strides, fast paced, but she had not slept well, so she shuffled slowly, head down. The milky ruffle of an oyster shell caught her eye and she bent to pick it up, then turned to the calm water and breathed in the silence. A dozen or more sanderlings skittered near her feet. Two swans, their huge wings negotiating with precision, flapped, flapped, and landed with webbed feet like water skis. She turned and picked up her pace, now marching. With the oyster shell in her left hand and her right hand open, she stretched her arms wide, then overhead, then back down to her sides. She breathed in the salt air and felt alive.

"I don't mean to invade your privacy," a startling baritone voice opened a door in the silence before she saw him, the tall man with the red hair.

"You did," she said, sharply, hardly recognizing her own voice. "I saw you come off the boat yesterday. Who are you?" It was not uncommon for islanders to talk to strangers, stranded folks or those lost in a place without written signs. More than forty years after the attack on the *SS Black Point* in the waters between the mainland and Harmony

Island, it was the weather that posed the greatest threat to islanders.

"Is that the way Harmony folks greet guests?"

He smiled, reached out his hand and said, "I'm Ricard."

"Ruth." She took his hand but was afraid of it. A warning shock sizzled along her hand then down her spine, like that which warns a dog of the boundary line in an invisible yard, the boundary that keeps it from danger.

"I saw you, too, sitting on the bench holding hands with your father. Was that your father?" With his white hair Andy did look older than his years, and she younger, but Andy would laugh to think someone thought he was her father.

"No, he's an old friend. How could you have seen me? You walked straight to your car."

"Boyfriend?" He pressed. How does one break the ice with a stranger, alone on a beach, where one doesn't belong? Did he know he'd find her here, a woman to fill a temporary void in his California life?

"No. Man friend. He runs the west side store. I've known him all my life."

"May I walk a way with you?" he asked, his bulk already sweeping her along.

Who knows how chemistry and situation intertwine to create an opening for decisions made quickly. Before the summer was over, Ruth married the red-haired and handsome Ricard with a baritone voice.

Eli was born within the first year. She and Rick argued fiercely about naming the child. Does the name determine the kind of man a child will become?

"He needs a strong name, like mine!" Like a stick on a drum, he snapped out the names, "Ricard, Jack, Kirk, or Spike."

"Spike!"

Ruth often watched the tide come in and she listened to its music. Her favorite sounds were soft like the breathing of the tide rising through Spartina along the shore. Spartina wouldn't be a fitting name, but maybe Eli. They would name their son Elymus, soul brother of Spartina. She loved the name. And, yes, she could see her son, a grown man, strong but willing to bend, like the grass for which he was named, resilient, fluid in movement.

"Eli," she said, later on the same day. "Eli will be his name."

Ricard gave in and they named the child Elymus, to be called Eli. He never argued with her again. Was it so devastating that their child had a name he could not savor? Was it that he had given in to her will and would not risk that again? Or was it that it didn't matter to him, after all?

It might not have mattered who came into the store after Ruth married Ricard. Though, the two of them lived just up the hill from Andy's store on the west shore, they might just as well have moved to California. He hardly saw Ruth anymore except on the rare occasions when she ran out of milk. They no longer played music together. Andy sat behind the counter, brooding.

"Hi, Sweetie," Laraine said, as she popped into the store again. She had come in only yesterday. "What's for dinner tonight?" she quipped, as she danced through the rigatoni and spaghetti sauce. It wasn't as though there was a huge selection.

"How old are you Andy?" she asked, one day, her long hair frizzed from humidity, her dress tight around her ample breasts. Laraine lived with two cats and a dog in a tiny rental, just south of Mid-island Avenue.

"What difference does it make, how old I am?" he said, with a twinkle in his eye. He liked Laraine. She was fun and sexy. Her spark appealed to him. These days he was so quiet and mellow, he felt he might drift out to sea on the next wave. He needed a spark in his life, not one that would send him hell bent to swim from shore to shore, but just one to keep him alive.

The bell jangled, and Ruth marched in with Eli in her arms. "Hi, Laraine. Andy, I just had to show you my beautiful Eli, this morning. Here, want to hold him, Grampa Andy? I can't believe I ran out of milk!"

Laraine moved in close, touching Andy with her shoulder in an attempt to see Eli better and, by the way, to breathe him in, this man Andy, so well known and well loved.

Ruth rested comfortably here in the moment, at the store with her friend Andy and neighbor Laraine. Only a tiny bit of her awareness remained up the hill with her husband. Ricard had come as a stranger to the island, a man without direction, floating between the continents of his life. He worked on the mainland for a California-based warehouse that distributed cooking supplies to better restaurants. He never intended to stay on the east coast.

Ruth had known little about Ricard when they married, but he was kind to her. "I love you, Ruth, and want you for my life," he had said. How lovely was their time together. He himself a cook, Ricard doted upon Ruth, especially as she cared for baby Eli. Sometimes at the end of the day after she laid Eli in his crib, she went into garden and picked oregano, sage, rosemary for the evening meal. He incorporated whatever she brought, even when he was already in the middle of making a special meal without them. A sign of his love, she thought.

But what is love and who decides? At what point does one become part of the fabric of a place? How do two people make a life together on an island or elsewhere?

"Do you feel lonesome without a child?" Laraine asked Andy, "Someone special to care for?" She milled around as she talked.

"Sometimes. Do you?" Andy scratched the back of his neck. He never asked personal questions, but here he was surprising himself, asking one.

"I've been sick all my life. I don't think about children much because I figured I'd never have one. I've got diabetes, high blood pressure, etc. You name it. I've got it, and I'm not even fifty years old." She spoke in a tone somewhere between braggadocio and mournfulness. "Kids love you, Andy. I see it."

"It's the penny candy." He smiled. If truth be told, since Eli's birth, Andy had felt a longing.

"Do you want to try making a child together?" The question shot out of her mouth like an arrow, which flamed and fell sweetly at Andy's feet. Laraine was a spitfire, always had been. She had bummed around with a hippie group, lived in a commune, experimented with mushrooms, while she was sleeping with a graduate student in mycology. Though it had ruined her health, she had done exactly what she had wanted to do.

A child. Andy sighed and said nothing.

A child binds two individuals and creates a reason for being. Andy knew about love, some kinds of love, (He would love Ruth forever, he knew that), but he wondered: If I had a child with Laraine, would I then love her, too?

Laraine continued to come into the store, almost every day. Sometimes she walked right over to the corned beef hash and worked her way around. To Dinty Moore's beef stew, all the while talking about the possibility of a child. Laraine had seen Andy with Ruth and occasionally, now, she saw Andy with Ruth's child. A tight little package would be her and Andy with child.

"O.K., Laraine," said Andy, one day. "I'm a little old for this, but let's try to make a baby."

Between shifts at the ferry dock, Jimmy Mahoney helped Laraine and Andy fix up the place. Joe Singleton, head tipped to one side, crooked body balanced from years of practice, steadied the ladder as Jimmy patched a hole where wet ceiling tiles had fallen through a couple of years ago during a torrential rain. The roof had been replaced, but the hole had remained. Andy hardly noticed it.

They moved boxes out of the storage room, painted the walls, hung lacy curtains, and fixed up the store to make it fit for a family. Laraine and Andy were married quietly on the mainland in a civil ceremony.

It wasn't hard for Laraine to get pregnant, but it was hard to carry the baby. She was diabetic and her numbers soared out of sight. She was in and out of the hospital to stabilize her diabetes. The last eight weeks of her pregnancy were spent on the mainland at her sister's house. Andy tended store on the island and saw her on Wednesday between the eight and ten o'clock boats. Joe Singleton watched the store during those hours. For neither Andy nor Laraine was it much of a marriage, two islanders now divided by illness. When Tommy was born, Laraine died.

Ruth had left her island teaching job a year ago when Eli was born. Now, each day she walked down the hill to help Andy with Tommy, his newborn son. She and Andy were a couple with two children and an unconsummated, undefined "marriage."

"Ruth, who are you married to?" Ricard asked, his red hair flaming as tension grew in their relationship.

"I'm sorry, Rick. I've taken energy from you for Andy and Tommy. But what can I do?" Ruth asked, already knowing the answer. She would do what she must do and that is take care of another man she loved and his son.

"Ricard's getting upset with me, Andy. I think he's jealous," she said when Tommy was six months old.

"Ruth, I can take care of Tommy, now I'm used to being with a baby. We do spend every night together. Let me ask questions. I'll do the rest myself." Andy said this with pride.

So Andy continued his education as a father in training. Sometimes Ruth even left Eli with Andy for an hour so that she and Ricard could be alone to remember the physical love that had been so important to them early in their relationship.

Jimmy, Joe, and other neighbors pitched in to help Andy. Louise, who lived at the south end, and her daughter Helen Mae came by. Helen Mae was five, and she loved taking the toddler Eli by the hand and walking him down the road and back. He was an easy child who would walk with anyone. Louise gave Tommy a bottle during that time. Jimmy put a car seat in the police cruiser and sometimes took Eli around the island on his runs. It wasn't long before Jimmy and his wife had a baby of their own. During those few years it was as though a tropical breeze carried baby pheromones through the air to the island.

Eli grew like a wisp of grass; Tommy was a blocky kid, even at four and five. They were pals. Years passed. Ruth struggled to keep a calm and contented household —

Ricard could be difficult — as Andy raised his child alone, with some help from the community, of course. Down at the dock, kids poked fun at Tommy and his father. "Is he your Grampa?" they would say. Father and son loved the bantering. Tommy crawled up on Andy's lap as they waited for groceries. Ruth and Andy shared their sons at the dock as they held hands waiting for groceries. Andy was Grampa Andy to Eli and all the island kids.

As they grew, he taught kids how to play both mandolin and guitar, his "legacy" to the island, he said with a twinkle in his eye. These were happy years for Andy, for Tommy, for Ruth and for Eli. Ricard worked off the island every day and spent weekends watching TV, feet on the couch, shoes still on. He'd push himself up heavily, grab a beer from the fridge, then sink back down.

Then during a bitterly cold January, after ten years of marriage, Ricard went to a trade show in San Francisco, "an opportunity to expand their lines to supplies for preparing Asian cuisine," he had said. He traveled to the West Coast on business and never came back. Ruth watched the sea smoke from her window and thought of the first time she had seen Ricard. It was summer, but he had reminded her of red sea smoke.

Eli was ten. He was a vulnerable wild child, devastated by the loss of his father. Eli raced around the island on his bicycle, always too fast, as if the wind would bring his father home or as if he could outrun his sadness. One day he disappeared. Ruth panicked and called Joe, who found him sitting on a rock on the west side.

Ricard never called. Never wrote. Once he touched down in San Francisco, he knew he would not return to

the island. He had family there. Another wife he had
abandoned ten years earlier. Children. Ruth would be fine,
and Eli, too. They had a community to support them. He
was a California guy. The kindest thing, he thought, was to
make a clean break — to disappear.

Ruth knew one of the companies with whom he did
business, and called to find out if they knew of him. Was
he all right? Had he had an accident? She had to be care-
ful. Didn't want to sound like a wife who had been left.
Yes. He came in periodically. Yes. He was working in San
Francisco full time now. They would leave a message.
He never called. It was as though he had fallen into the San
Andreas Fault and been swallowed whole.

Andy was there to listen, day after day. And always
there was the music. She loved to sing with him. On the
mandolin Andy strummed while she picked out the melody. They'd switch, he playing the melody, she strumming.
Sometime when the music welled up and filled the room,
he chimed in and sang a little harmony.

What is it that marks a life for its duration? That
causes it to make a left turn or an about face, so that one
closes in or breaks out? Is it an aborted chance at being
a hero? Is it the loss of one's parents, a husband, wife or
child? Is it love? Or music?

"Sit down, boys," Andy said. "Eli, you've learned to
play 'Down in the Valley' one way. Tommy, you've learned
it another way. Let's hear you play it together." Through
music, he tried desperately to tame the boys. As Tommy
grew, Andy was haunted by his own foolishness at sixteen.
He never told Tommy the story of bragging about his
swimming or about the fifty-dollar bet to swim across the

channel, and Pete's disappearance. That shocking day, however, had marked his life and was always close to the surface of his parenting.

Early in the summer when Eli was sixteen and Tommy fifteen, they became "camp counselors" on the island. They advertised on Andy's store bulletin board: "Kid sitting, Saturday mornings, kids 6-8. Call E and T." They led the kids in a camp counseling way. They took them hiking at the south end and at the north end, and they taught them how to bait a hook and drop a fish line from the wharf. And Eli and Tommy prepared ahead for a day it might rain. They created a magnet project with the kids.

On that day of rain, for which they had prepared, they were allowed to use the one-room schoolhouse, where they set up a table with magnets and iron filings. Four little kids, ages six through eight, three boys and a girl, gathered round the table. "Hey, Eli," Tommy said. It was the 'Hey, Eli,' that always got them into trouble. "Let's see how that magnet looks in your nose." Later, Eli would understand that the incident was a precursor to the accident, which happened later that summer. He was so willing to please. Was that it? He could not resist the request, or was it the challenge?

Later that day, they worked on Andy's Whaler.

"The barnacles around the motor and on the bottom of the boat will slow her down, boys," Andy said. "Always keep the bottom of your boat clean."

"Eli, you scrape, I'll polish," said Tommy. "Gotta build that muscle of yours." Whenever they worked or played their bantering rattled incessantly. Tommy was the boss, the muscle man; Eli the brain, the skinny kid, willing to please.

"As you say, Sir," he said with a smile. And they worked the rest of the day until the twenty-year-old Whaler looked like new.

Most islanders moored their boats on the east side of the island, the same side from which Andy and Pete had launched their swim oh so many years ago. The eastern shore of the island was closest to the mainland. Andy's mooring sat one hundred feet from shore below Joe Singleton's house, south of Salem's Point lighthouse and west of the red nun channel marker. He kept an eight-foot dinghy on the beach for transport back and forth, from shore to boat.

"She's ready to go back on the mooring now," said Andy. "Eli, you drive my truck and you, boys, moor the boat. Make her secure, Tommy. You know how. I can't help saying it again, boys. Just two rules: Always ask before you take the boat out and always remember safety first."

Teen years short circuit good intentions of those with the brawniest of bodies and the brightest of minds. At midnight, two weeks before the start of school, Eli and Tommy took the boat without permission. They were fooling around in Andy's Whaler, when Eli at the wheel slammed the boat into the red nun channel marker on the east side of the island. Tommy catapulted into the black nighttime water and disappeared.

On the island's east side overlooking the bay and the red nun, Joe Singleton could not sleep. His body ached and he was hot. Even before he rolled off his bed and leaned on the bedside chair cranking himself up for a drink of water, he'd heard the whine of a boat's engine, not like the deep groan of freight carrier engines churning up the dark channel, but more of a high keening. He heard the boys shouting, and now only one screaming voice, desperate, "Tommy! Tommy!" He dialed 911.

In the early hours of the morning fire fighters and rescue volunteers set up searchlights along Salem's Light beach. As with any island event from the Firemen's Fair to hurricane cleanup, neighbors turned out. They combed the shoreline on foot and from small boats. A Coast Guard boat roared up from the mouth of the bay to search the channel for Tommy.

Andy, Eli, Ruth, Jimmy Mahoney, and a few others crammed into Ruth's warm kitchen. The smell of coffee nauseated Andy. To cope, he required solitude. His hand on the countertop, he eased away from the others, backing toward the door. Questions roared in his head until he felt a surge of angry energy so strong that he knew he could race out the door and hurt someone in his way. "No, Ruth!" He resisted her hugging arms, threw them off, as he lurched toward the door.

"Andy, I'm sorry," she said.

He opened the door and slammed it behind him. Through the window she saw him trudge down the hill toward home.

Jimmy Mahoney dialed up Joe Singleton. "Joe, I need your help," he said. I don't want Andy to be alone tonight. Could you grab your sleeping bag and go down to his place 'til morning." When he was three years old, Joe Singleton had fallen down a flight of stairs. He lived with physical and mental disabilities as a result of the injury. But those limitations were normal to him now, and though his spine was crooked and his head tilted to one side, and though he had a hard time getting out the words he wanted to say, he felt normal. Even neighbors whom he'd know for years, tried to protect him. A few, like Jimmy, understood that he was as capable in many ways as anyone else. "Sure, Jimmy, I go right away," he said.

Jimmy Mahoney with teenaged kids of his own, forced himself to remain calm and warm, but businesslike. He found himself rubbing his balding head, which he did when he was shaken. It could have been his Jim, also smack in the middle of the crazy teens. In a tiny room off the kitchen, he questioned Eli, who stood, rigid, against the wall. Jimmy took notes to file his accident report.

"What happened, Eli?" Jimmy had lived year round on the island with his wife Elaine, since they were married sixteen years ago. Jim was their only son, born when Eli was about two years old. He had known Eli all his life, as a good kid, compliant, but wild with his father Ricard gone now for, what was it, six years.

"A game. It was a game. Touch the Nun," Eli said. "First his turn to drive. Then mine," Words stuck in his throat even while details played like a crazy film stuck on one image — Tommy flying out of the boat. Officer Mahoney wrote a few notes. "I screwed up. Hit the red nun."

"You were in Andy's boat, right?" Jimmy knew Andy would never allow the boys to take the boat at night.

"We weren't supposed to take it without permission. But we did." Eli couldn't say it was Tommy who wanted to play the game. Eli had been nervous about taking the boat right from the beginning. "He'll kill us, Tommy," he'd said. "You'll be grounded for a month." Tommy was fifteen, but Andy was tough on him, kept him reigned in. "Hey, Eli, next week you'll be gone," Tommy had said. Back at school. "Come on, Eli, what are you getting to be a wimpy fucking prep school kid?" The dig. Tommy still attended the island school. Only ten kids, grades seven through twelve. "O.K., you bum, let's do it," Eli had said.

The accident, the ongoing search, neighbors in the house, Jimmy asking questions ever so gently, Andy, Eli. Her son, Eli. By four in the morning Ruth fell into bed, like a sack of stones. Do accidents just happen? She wondered. Or in the string of events of a young life does the weaver (Who is the weaver?) drop a stitch, pick up an alien color, or lose concentration? She fell into a hard sleep.

Ruth awoke thinking of Eli's father Ricard, who had come as a stranger to the island. As a physical presence, he disappeared from their lives even as he remained in Eli's genes and Ruth's dreams. Andy had helped her to heal, to understand her own anger and sadness. Now she ached for her son and wanted to blame Ricard for Tommy's death. She needed Andy's help. Andy had become a surrogate father to her son, but how could she or Eli now look Andy in the eye?

Eli could not sleep. As he walked down the hill at four thirty in the morning, the image of Tommy flying out of the boat became entangled, like a monster fish caught with multiple hooks and lines. Anger, loss, guilt. He wanted to scream, to blame, but most of all, he wanted to hear his friend's voice. He saw Joe Singleton's car at Andy's and saw shadows moving in Andy's house. He kept on walking.

Suddenly Tommy was there and they were laughing like fiends. The details lurched in his head. It was earlier in the summer when they were sitters or "camp counselors" for little kids and it was raining. They had decided to do the magnet project. Eli had brought his collection of magnets to the schoolhouse for the project, magnets ranging from bar magnets to iron filings from Joe Singleton's father's machine shop and a half dozen bullet shaped magnets, magnetized hematite, given to him by his great uncle who was a geologist. The kids had gathered round the table.

Eli remembered becoming a tall stick-moving clown.
He stuck one of the small bullet-shaped magnets in his
nose to amuse the kids. Actually, he remembered now, it
was Tommy who'd said, "Hey, Eli, let's see how that magnet looks in your nose," and he handed him the magnet.
Whenever Tommy said, "Hey, Eli," Eli knew there'd be an
adventure — or trouble. A couple of kids had started to
giggle. He bent to the table and grasped another magnet
and put it into the other nostril. He barked like a walrus.
But the magnets slipped a little too high into his nose and
they stuck together. He panicked. "Tommy, get me some
pliers," he said through a mix of fear and laughter."

This was the summer of Tommy's nose ring. "Are you
kidding? I'm not getting near you. Do you think I'm
going to get stuck nose to nose with a human walrus. The
children were rolling on the floor laughing. Eli imagined
the rescue squad coming to take him away to the hospital
with magnets moving up his nose toward his brain. In his
panic, he forgot that he could take another strong magnet
and pull them out. "Come on, Tommy, the pliers."

And Tommy, making a big show of it all, pulled the
magnets out one by one. Eli sat the kids down and admitted that he had done a stupid thing. "Look, you guys, even
to be funny, don't ever put anything into your nose.
I wanted to be the clown and I loved hearing you laugh,
but it was foolish. Don't do that, O.K.? I promise I won't
do anything like that again, either." For the first time in his
life, Eli knew that he needed to think before he acted.

The west side of the island is the wild side, undevel-
oped, pristine. There, Eli laughed and cried then sobbed
until he was exhausted and could hardly see. He paced the

shoreline and he laughed again at Tommy flourishing the pliers like a mad long-haired dentist poised to remove his walrus tusks. Mad dentist. Maybe I'll just go insane, I won't have to live with this. Did I think before I acted, the way I said I would? What now?

Ruth popped awake, got up to go to the bathroom and opened Eli's bedroom door, slowly, on the way back to her room. He was not there. Down the hill she saw lights on at Andy's. Joe Singleton's car was still there. She called on the phone. Joe picked it up. "How's Andy doing, Joe? Is Eli there?"

"Andy's quiet. No, Ruthie, Eli is not here. I'm going to the ferry dock. I'll look for him along the way. He probably needs to be soothed by the island. You know, they way he is."

"I do know, Joe, thanks for reminding me." Ruth flashed back to the times after Ricard had left when Eli had been missing. Joe had found him, sitting on a rock looking out at the water. More than once Joe and Jimmy Mahoney had calmed her down and located Eli.

"I'll come around that way again to drop some groceries off to Andy. I'll stop by, O.K.?"

"Thanks, Joe, I'll have the coffee on."

Around the corner came Joe Singleton's Ford pickup, sleeping bag in the bag in the back. "Hey, Eli, I'm on my way over to meet the six o'clock ferry. Want to ride along? I might need your help, picking up Andy's order. He wants to open the store today." Keeping busy was the only way that Andy could survive as the search for Tommy continued.

"O.K."

"You look like hell. Think you can get a little sleep after we drop off Andy's stuff?"

"Maybe, I'm pretty tired." A little piece of Eli was ready to spill all his feelings to Joe. He wanted to say he might not be able to live. That he never had wanted to take the boat. That he'll probably always be talked into things that he didn't want to do. That he's a danger in the world. Weak. That he's a fuckup and probably always would be. That Andy was so great and now how could he look at him. He wasn't even sure he could sit in the car when they drove by Salem's Point lighthouse. The search for Tommy was still going on. He knew by the way the current was running and the tide that Tommy was long gone. They wouldn't find him. Tommy. Jesus. And to face Ruth, his mother. He realized Joe was talking, as if he were reading Eli's mind.

"Can I talk to you straight, Eli?" Joe said, his head flopped to one side, more than the usual.

"Yeah, Joe, I guess so,"

"You've got two weeks before you go back to school. You fucked up. And now you have to decide what to do. You're not the only one, you know. We all fucked up. Maybe, some of us have been lucky, and we haven't lost a friend in the bargain, but we've all been there. We've hurt those we love. I could make a list of the stories I know, but I won't. You're hearing me, right?"

Eli didn't know if he could tolerate Joe's mini-lecture. But another piece of him needed to hear it. He looked at the twisted body behind the wheel and thought about how Joe's parents must have felt after he fell down the stairs. Maybe Joe was talking about that now without mentioning names, or maybe not. "I'm hearing you, Joe."

They swung around the corner ready to take a left into the ferry parking lot. Joe was looking at Eli, Eli at the car coming straight at them, ready to pull into the lot, and poised for a head on collision. Thena, looking beautiful and terrified behind the wheel of her mother Louise's ancient Volkswagen bug slammed on her brakes as Joe continued on into the lot. Eli smiled. "Jesus, Joe, you almost got us killed."

"I knew she'd stop," he said, as though he had just sliced through soft butter, "She loves you. We all love you, Eli."

Two weeks after the accident, despite Joe's statements of love, and despite his mother Ruth's tenderness, Eli felt miserable, unworthy of love. He sat with his bags around him, ready to return to school, except for the nagging guilt that he'd been carrying around with him. He was so full of the story playing around in his mind, that he was desperate to share it with Andy and ask his forgiveness. Just to sit with him quietly would be enough.

Andy moped around the store, straightening out shelves. He looked at his mandolin, hanging on a rack like a rusty gun, empty and without purpose. He had no energy to do anything. He knew it was not Eli who was at fault. It was the fact of being sixteen. Even so, he was unable to break the barrier standing between Eli and him, and, therefore, between Ruth and him.

The bell jangled as Eli opened the door. "'Morning, Andy, I..."

Like a blind man, Andy turned toward Eli, then not seeing the boy, turned and walked into the back room leaving Eli alone. Inside the back room, he sat on his cot, hunched over and cried.

The bell jangled as Eli left the store. He wanted so much to hug Andy, to tell him the story of what happened, to say I'm sorry. The west side tugged at him, the wild place, where he ordinarily went for screaming out loud or for healing, but he resisted the pull and moped up the hill toward home and his mother.

"Eli, why didn't you follow him into the back room?" said Ruth.

"Mom, no one goes back there. You know that," said Eli.

"We choose our own boundaries, Eli, and sometimes you have to cross over, climb over the rocks and brave falling into the chasm. Sometimes we have to act in order to save ourselves — and our friends. Andy needs you to say I'm sorry."

"And what about you, Mom. Have you talked to Andy?" Even at sixteen, Eli rarely challenged his mother.

"No, she said, "I feel a wall between Andy and the living world."

The next day Eli went off to school. Ruth called ahead to the headmaster, explained what had happened, and requested grief counseling for Eli.

The route towards forgiveness forks, then rises up the great mountain with hairpin turns and boulders threatening to fall into the road, blocking passage. Still, the way exists.

In the first September storm, the wind howled and rain slammed against the south windows of the store as Andy dressed in the blue blazer he hadn't worn since his wedding.

He packed his leather slouch with maps he had studied and bus schedules he's sent for. He thought of his orienteering training with the Navy Seals. It'a all about stamina and attitude, the training officer had said. Over his slacks and blazer, he donned his foul weather gear, put the pack on the chair and went out the door. He was a stranger to the mainland, but Andy prepared the way for a visit to Eli at his school, just south of Boston.

He had a list:

1) Leave store by 7:45 for ferry at 8:30
2) Take 8:30 ferry to town.
3) Take bus from town to city. (9:15)
4) Train from city to Boston. (10:30)
5) Subway from Boston to school.
6) Call Eli. (He'd penciled in Maybe this should be #3 or #1).

Andy was nervous, so nervous he almost forgot his leather sack. He'd closed the store for the first time in years and walked up the road, reviewing the steps of his plan when he remembered the sack on the chair and had to go back.

In the rain and wind, he felt alive, hopeful, that he'd see Eli. He'd hold his hands the way he and Ruth had held hands for so many years. (But not since Tommy's death, he now realized.) Maybe that would be enough. He might not be able to say the words, "I forgive you, Eli" not because he didn't forgive Eli but because it was much more compli-cated than that.

"I guess it begins with forgiving myself," he said out loud.

"For what?" he challenged himself. Might he cry there on the road on the way to the ferry on the way to Eli on the way to what?

"For making a baby who would never reach sixteen? A baby carrying my crazy genes?" But how he had loved Tommy. And the rest of the kids who came into the store for penny candy and who called him Grampa Andy.

There along Mid-island Road on his way to the ferry, he talked to himself. Like a friend, he thought. He turned left onto the main drag and saw Salem Point Lighthouse and the red nun off to the right. He flashed back to the guys at the Searchlight Unit. "Cripes, how cocky I was!" he says out loud. "And stupid."

In his mind he recreated what must have been the scene with Eli and Tommy. He'd like to hear the whole story. Or maybe not. The boat. The game. Did Tommy talk Eli into the game? Wasn't he usually the instigator? Eli's a lot like me, he thought. Wild and gentle. Pete had died. Wasn't I just as much at fault as if I was driving a boat? Weren't they both innocent of evil intent? The two stories, over fifty years apart, intertwined and knotted up. The southeast winds howled. "Must be forty knots," Andy said aloud. He pulled the hood of his foul weather gear closer to his face and didn't hear the car come up behind him.

"Hey, Andy. What the hell you doin' out here? Get in."

"Talking to myself in the rain," Andy said. "I'm taking the 8:30 ferry."

Joe Singleton was on his way to the boat to see if the morning papers were coming in. "Do you think it will run?"

"It has to. I've got business on the other side," said Andy.

Jimmy Mahoney sat in his police vehicle as he did four times a day at boat times, at the ferry dock, where neighbors gather. The place was deserted. Jimmy got out of his vehicle and walked over to Joe's car. "The ferry's not running," he said.

Upon his arrival at school, Eli had received a note to attend a meeting with the Grief Counselor. He'd been having nightmares, kept waking up, then overslept. The Counselor said, "Tell me what happened, as if it is happening now, in the present tense. That's the first step, to say it out loud."

As if in a trance, Eli raised his head and gazed into the place, at midnight, under the light of Salem's Point Lighthouse. "Tommy and me, I, are fooling around. We're laughing like fools. We're in the Whaler. It's a great little boat. It's black out there, blacker than a.... Well, anyway, we're trying to see who can come closest to the red nun. You can't see the marker until you're practically on top of it.

"He gets first shot. It's hi…his boat. I'm standing at the bow. When he zooms by the marker I try to touch it. Tommy's too far away. A little chicken…" Eli swallowed a sob.

"Now, it's my turn. I can't even see the channel marker. It's so dark. I'm afraid to go too fast until I see it. I give it the gas and Tommy leans out to touch the nun. We're laughing our asses off. 'I think I touched it,' he says, which is kind of funny because it means a point for me. Then he gets behind the wheel. We do this back and forth. We're playing to six. The first one getting close enough for six touches wins. I know how Andy'd hate Tommy fooling around in the boat. I should call it quits. But I can't 'cause we're revved.

"We're tied at five to five. Now, I'm at the wheel again. This time, I say to myself, once I see the marker I'm going for the center, then at the last minute I'll veer off so we'll actually hit it, but barely, like a scrape. We'll bump off it. I'll be the winner, for sure.

"I'm scared, though, because I know I'll have to turn away quick. Tommy's at the bow screaming with joy, 'Come on, you fucker,' he says, and his hair's flying in the wind." Eli worked his throat to get rid of the lump. " I lean on the throttle, and the red nun pops up right in front of me. I swear she put out a red finger and grabbed the boat. He screams scared and it's too late. Before I can turn the wheel, he's flying out of the boat, like a bird. Then he's gone.

"I'm shaking and feeling crazy, circling round and round, thinking he'll come up. I remember the spotlight Andy rigged up on a car battery. And I shine that thinking I'll find him, bobbing like a cork. But I kind of know he won't come up. I keep screaming his name, screaming and screaming." Eli shrieked the words like the keening of a tribal mourner. "For awhile, I think I'm going crazy. I keep seeing the nun, him flying out of the boat, and he's screaming in my head." Eli looked at the counselor, his black hair springing straight out from his head, his face contorted in pain. "Our friend, Joe Singleton heard us and dialed 911. A lot of people came to help, but they couldn't do anything. It was too late."

On the island later that same day, the wind shifted around and by late afternoon a dry breeze blew from the

northwest. Ruth sat on the hill. Inside the store Andy
picked up his mandolin, dusted it off with the corner of his
shirt, and sat on a stool. To the west the sun was setting,
not a roiling sunset like the night before, but a burnished
red golden ball. The water shimmered molten silver and
gold. Ruth's dark eyes gleamed as Andy, an old man with
balding white hair, picked out silent music below. She
whispered, "All right, my friend, tonight's the night. Let's
break down this wall of silence!" She patted her rock, got
up to walk the hill toward her house, and kissed her hand
to the rising moon.

Inside, she gently lifted her guitar from its stand,
slipped her pick into the pocket of her jeans, and marched
as only Ruth can march, an older woman now, hair still
dark, swinging back and forth, out the door with the guitar
in hand.

Now, suddenly, the whole world moved in slow motion
in the satin glow of twilight. She glided, almost floated,
as in a dream. Below her, on the stool in the darkened
store and clearly silhouetted against the setting sun, Andy
plucked his mandolin, alone.

Ruth slipped onto the porch and settled herself onto
the bench facing the water and a glint of the setting sun
just visible now above the horizon. The song he played was
familiar and her fingers found the chords. She accompanied
him, she on the outside, he on the inside, the wall between.
But it was all the same, their music, one song. He slipped
into "Isle au Haut" and the two played. Softly, she sang the
words:"

If I could give you three things,
I would give you these.

Song and laughter and a wooden home
On the shining seas.*

The music stopped and the door opened. Andy held his
mandolin in one hand, the open door in the other. Ruth
arose and entered. He put out his hand to help her. Without a word, she sat on the stool he had moved into place
so that she faced him, almost knee to knee. They played
together and she sang:

Sleep where the wind is warm
And the moon is high
Give sadness to the stars
Sorrow to the sky.

When you see old Isle au Haut
Rising in the dawn
You will play in the yellow fields
In the morning sun.

He paused in the melody and she picked it up, her
instrument more lyrical, deeper sounding, than his. Now he
played the tune in harmony. In all the years of their music
together, she had never heard him play this way.

When did he learn this harmony without words? She
wondered and looked up. His forehead creased, he smiled
at her, a sad smile from *the depths of an ocean of experience*
playing in his sparkly eyes. She plucked the strings of her
guitar, an interlude, and he received her gift as she repeated
the melody.

*From the song "Isle au Haut Lullabye," words and music by Gordon Bok, copyrighted in 1965. Reprinted here with permission.

—the depths of an ocean of experience —

Those of us who live on Harmony Island, or in any community, where we have the privilege of living with our elders, are blessed. Here is just one little story from my "living" with Marcy.

At the Store

Marcy sits at the table in the back room of the store. There she works, head bent over, gray banana curls bobbing. From that spot she can see the cash register and the counter. There she talks with neighbors who come in to wait for the ferry or who buy a piece of pizza and sit at the table to eat.

On this day, she is alone. "Have you read Todd's book yet?" I asked. Joe Bains and John Thresher edited Todd Farnham's papers after he died. They published a small book through the Historical Society.

"Yes," she said, "but I'm disappointed. It doesn't mention Mary, or Molly or Millie. It doesn't even talk much about the Farm."

"So are you saying it doesn't have heart?" I said.

"Yeah, that's what I want my stories to have." She lowered her head and smiled. Marcy and I have been talking about her stories for twenty-six years.

"Are you ready to start writing them? Neither of us is getting any younger," I said. Marcy is eighty-four years old.

"Oh, I've scribbled some down, but nobody will ever be able to read my writing. I keep thinking I'll get going on them, then I say, maybe another day."

"Marcy," I said, hearing myself getting insistent, "you can't wait to be inspired. One day maybe it would be good to say, 'O.K. today we'll begin.' You know I'll help you." She looked at me and smiled again, that smile that says everything and nothing.

Then she began a little story:

When the Army camp was mid island, the ration ship would come in. Madame Alice would see it come in and call up to the Army Camp so they'd know they had to get ready fast for a white-glove inspection.

But they had a wood stove! How could they prepare that for a white glove inspection? She asks, rhetorically and grinning widely.

A neighbor came into the store. Marcy rang a quart of milk at the cash register. Then she sat again at the long table.

How I wanted to ask her to say more. What exactly was a ration ship? How did she know that Madame Alice called the men? Was Danny at the Army camp then (She eventually married Danny)? "Tell me more," I wanted to say. But the moment was gone.

"Thanks, Marcy," I said, for sharing your little story," then I went on my way.

As I walked away from the store, I thought of the goldmine of stories that Marcy stores from a lifetime on the island. Then, I laughed aloud, thinking of a story of my own about Marcy.

One day she and I talked about living and dying on the island. We both agreed that we wanted to be cremated and buried here.

"I want to be buried in the Historical Cemetery," she said, referring to the tiny cemetery mid island.

"How is that going to happen?" I said, thinking of the formalities that must happen in order for a simple citizen of the twenty-first century, like you or me, to be buried there.

"It's easy," she said. "Just *dig a little hole and bury my ashes* there."

I laughed.

"I'll bury yours there if you bury mine," she said.

—dig a little hole and bury my ashes —
"Pink" is a work of fiction.

Pink

"Your father wanted to be cremated, his ashes sprinkled
in the herb garden outside this kitchen window," said
Louise, looking first at Thena's smooth face, then at Helen
Mae's. The three women sat at the round kitchen table on
the morning after Ralph's death. If they could all touch the
circle, maybe they'd connect, Louise thought. Helen Mae's
hands remained in her lap. Her husband Jack finished drying the morning dishes and stood leaning on the kitchen
counter, near the sink and the curtain-framed window overlooking the herb garden.

That garden is shaped like a fish, its head closest to the
window, the tail, further up or back. Ralph had said it was
a fish standing on its nose, a fish with a lavender head and a
tall feathery valerian tail, with German chamomile, lavender, sage, echinacea purpurea, and thyme flanking the sides.
To the left of the fish are parsley, chives, and rosemary.
From this garden, Louise made teas to calm both Ralph and
her during their last days together.

"Mother, sometimes your quirkiness goes a little beyond reason," said Helen Mae, the willowy eldest daughter
and Ralph's stepchild. "Why can't we just have a traditional burial here on the island, you know, with a 'Here lies
Ralph...' tombstone?" She twisted the ends of her sandy
blonde hair, just as she had when she was a child. Helen
Mae, along with her sister Thena, had grown up mid island.
With her husband Jack, Helen Mae now rented one of the

renovated Navy barracks at the south end of Harmony Island.

Helen Mae stood up, towering over her childlike mother. "He wanted to have his ashes buried in the herb garden because *you* wanted that," she said, making her point as much with her blonde hair and her whole body as with her words. How hard it was to understand her mother and the relationship with her stepfather. She had never been able to enter their world.

Ralph's daughter Thena, almond eyes, olive skin, looked pensively at Louise. Then she turned to Helen Mae. "I don't know," she said. "What exactly did my father want?" Thena had driven from Maine to Rhode Island, and taken the ferry from the mainland to the island, to be with her family during Ralph's final moments. At two in the morning, Ralph had passed away. Thena called Hospice, who sent a nurse over on the Fire and Rescue Boat to pronounce him dead. The island policeman arrived to do his part. Because six hours would elapse before the morning ferry, the Fire Chief allowed the body to be transported — along with the Hospice nurse — to the mainland aboard the rescue boat. Thena stayed with Louise as they made arrangements for Ralph's burial.

You'd think the burying part would be easy, thought Louise. But it isn't. Holding onto the table for support, Louise rose, too, and reached out her small hand to touch Helen Mae, who moved just out of reach toward her husband Jack. Like a preacher at prayer service, Louise spread both her arms wide and said, "Ralph wanted the garden. So do I."

Still seated at the table, Thena nodded.

And that was that.

Ralph was cremated. In every other respect the funeral was traditional for the island, with friends gathering for calling hours on the mainland and later with the procession from the ferry parking lot up to Louise's house, mid island near Wampanoag Spring and the ancient burial ground. In two's and three's islanders trudged up the hill, dressed in fleece or wool caps, winter jackets, mittens and warm boots as the late March wind blew from the northeast. Outdoors, standing in a circle, rosy cheeked island friends wept and spoke, then chuckled, about the living Ralph, his black curly hair, his grand strong hugging arms, and his black boot poised to kick a drinking friend out the door.

Ralph had played the accordian in a lively island music group. His friend, Old Benny, played a mean fiddle. The only musical instrument Louise had tried was harmonica. Though she loved the fast tempo of "Roll in My Sweet Baby's Arms," she could play only flute-like notes in melancholy songs. Now Old Benny lifted his fiddle and teased out of that quivering instrument the beautiful "Danny Boy."

Louise did not weep. In her love for Ralph, she wore bright green, like new leaves unfolding. She had already grieved her loss as Ralph lay dying in a hospital bed, set up in their living room, where he watched the birds close up at the feeder and glimpsed the shipping traffic down the bay's east passage in the distance. Louise stood in the circle smiling, serene within her own world. What is deceased? She asked herself, as voices droned in the distance. Ralph dead and gone? No. Deceased is a special kind of dormant. Like plants in the garden. Aren't we the same, really? A period of sleep or low activity follows the departure from this life, then who knows how or where Ralph would burst into the world.

What fun it would be if a man dressed in a grocer's apron suddenly arrived upon the scene in the produce section of the market as she picked over slightly mushy end-of-the-winter McIntosh apples, and he said, "Hey Louise, Baby, (Oops, can I still call you Baby?) I used to be Ralph." Hmm. How would that work, though? Louise shook her head as if to shift the pieces of the puzzle inside it from one picture to another. Could the reincarnated Ralph be a fully-grown man or would he have to be a new baby? Or might he be self-seeded chamomile in the garden? She felt Helen Mae's eyes on her. Louise had been smiling while others wept, and she felt the tension between disapproval and curiosity from her first daughter, the one born before Louise understood love.

Love. A few weeks after Ralph's funeral, for the purpose of settling her own estate before Louise went in for hip surgery, (which didn't alarm Louise, but which did concern Helen Mae), the family gathered this time in the office of Louise's lawyer. There was Louise, wife of the deceased Ralph and owner of their combined estates; Helen Mae, Louise's first daughter, born of a brief marriage when Louise was in her early twenties, Helen Mae, now thirty-five and married for three years to Jack, a free-lance construction worker whom she met while she was working as a clerk at Ace Hardware on the mainland; and Thena, thirty year-old daughter of Ralph, a fund raiser for nonprofit organizations, single and owner of her own home in Portland, Maine. This is the cast of characters, the small family that assembled on a bright April morning to assuage Helen Mae's anxiety before her mother's hospital admittance.

Lawyer's offices ordinarily do not spawn statements of love. Chairs and a mahogany table. Dark, sun-blocking drapes on the windows. Stiff portraits on the walls. "Love is my legacy," Louise said, when everyone was seated. "Whatever else we decide here should be determined in the name of love."

"You can't divide up love," Helen Mae said, impatient with her mother's refusal to be practical. Jack covered Helen Mae's hand with his. He loved the soft wisdom of Louise and the awkward insecurity of her daughter Helen Mae. Thena smiled at Helen Mae, then at Louise. "I'm sure there's enough to go around," she said. "We're a small family." All of this legal settling is unnecessary, she thought. Twenty years from now when mother dies, we could easily share what she has left.

"What if Jack and I break up?" Helen Mae asked. Jack felt a twinge as he considered the frowning portrait hanging behind and slightly above his wife. His hand remained on hers. No one addressed the question. With the help of her lawyer and with consensus of the family, Louise decided that Helen Mae would inherit Louise's small house. She named Thena beneficiary on her insurance policy and gave Thena her favorite of Louise's baskets and the framed photograph of Salem's Point Lighthouse. Louise said Jack could have the rest of her baskets and her paintings by island artists. Jack dabbled in oils. For Louise's birthday, he had painted her front porch, with a special slant of sun. It was the first time anyone had ever painted for her. The business matter offered peace of mind to Helen Mae and, in a formal way, conveyed Louise's love. The papers would be drawn up within a few days and signed by all parties. For Louise the legal matter had nothing to do with dying.

Electing hip surgery is testimony to the urge for life. Dressed in brown slacks and a lime shirt, Louise settled into her chair at the kitchen table, on the morning of her hospital admission. Strands of dampened lily leaves lay on the table. She hummed "Amazing Grace" as she chose three strands and twisted them into a thin rope, both as a meditation and a beginning for her next basket. She breathed in the fluting call of the red-winged blackbird, then the entryway door slammed and Helen Mae darted into the room. Louise caught the heightened energy and let it go. "Good morning, Honey," she said. "Sit down while I finish my tea."

Helen Mae stood. "Jack forgot to put gas in the car, I thought we'd be late for the ferry, what time do we have to be at the hospital?" She plucked the teacup from her mother's hand and set it on the counter.

As Helen Mae reached for her mother's elbow to help her up, she knocked Louise, with a wince, off balance. She stretched both arms and caught the smaller woman, but they landed with a thud in an awkward embrace. The two women lying half under the kitchen table, their faces inches apart, looked at each other in a frozen moment. The window over the kitchen sink slammed shut, disarming and opening them to a burst of shared laughter. "Well," Louise said, her head resting on Helen Mae's arm, "That's the finest hug I've had since you were twelve years old!"

The day was a breath of springtime softness. Louise watched the morning clouds draw back while Helen Mae drove her ten-year-old island car onto the ferry, then off on the mainland, and as she chauffeured her mother to County General Hospital. Louise hummed to calm herself and her daughter, but the humming aggravated Helen Mae, so that by the time they reached the hospital a half hour later she was ready to throttle her incessantly upbeat mother.

Helen Mae remained with her mother to be sure the admission process was handled properly. As though they were at a cocktail party, Louise happily introduced her daughter to Barbara, the friendly nurse's aide she herself had just met, and to the orthopedic surgeon who had operated on Ralph's knees, twice, and who now stood talking with another doctor as she was wheeled down the salmon and cream hallway.

At the admissions desk, without hesitation, Louise signed the customary release form, informing the patient of the possibility of death as a result of anesthesia and releasing the hospital of liability. She passed it along for Helen Mae to read and sign. With no word between them, Helen Mae and her mother acknowledged that under anesthesia Louise could die. A hand closed around Helen Mae's throat. Her mother, the flesh and blood woman she had held in her arms under the kitchen table minutes ago, could die. She looked at Louise who held her usual peaceful, slightly amused expression. For only the second time in her thirty-five years of life (Had she been sleeping through Ralph's demise?), Helen Mae acknowledged the reality of death.

Helen Mae wondered at her own childishness when she thought of the possible imminent death of her mother and as she flashed back to the death of her dog. It seemed absurd to compare the two. Helen Mae's father had walked away from home when she was two years old. Her only memory was her father standing beside her dead dog by the side of a paved road, with a sidewalk. Which road? Not on the island, where roads are gravel. In her memory she saw her father nudge with his sneakered foot her snuggly dog Skip.

What is different is often suspect. Helen Mae did not know another adult male in her life during those early years, until she turned five and Ralph came on the scene, Ralph a big huggable man so physical he frightened her. He spread his arms wide for her to come inside, she ran

toward him, but at the last minute Helen Mae ducked and
hid. When a stray dog found them one day at the beach and
moved into their island home, Helen Mae screamed when
Ralph went near the dog.

How confusing was the world of dogs and men and love
to the young Helen Mae!

Ralph and Louise loved unabashedly. At night in their
cozy living room Louise turned out all the lights, she sat
on Ralph's lap and traced the bones of his face, the sock-
ets around his eyes, his cheekbones, his jaw, the line of his
nose, his full lips. Before he finished tracing her face, they
fell into each other's arms laughing at the wonder of having found each other. Eventually this love play in the dark
became their ritual gift to each other. Louise said that she
wanted to develop muscle memory, so that if Ralph died
before she did, he'd still be there in her muscles.

One night when Louise and Ralph were playing blind
love, Helen Mae got up from her bed and shuffled out of
her room. The nightlight was not on, but she could hear
soft laughter from the living room. She flicked on the light
at the top of the stairs and caught her mother and Ralph on
the couch, her mother on Ralph's lap. Why did they have
the light out? What were they doing in the dark? Louise
called Helen Mae to come sit with them, and the child
padded down the stairs to the couch where they remained,
Louise on Ralph's lap. "Our touching each other is another
way of knowing," she said, and she invited Helen Mae
to close her eyes and touch their faces. "Pretend that you
do not have eyes to see, but that your fingertips are your
eyes," she said. Helen Mae, closed her eyes, and reached
out a little, then pulled back as though she had touched a
hot woodstove. She could not join them. Her mother who
had always held her when she cried, seemed different with

Ralph. Helen Mae twisted her long hair and chewed on the end of it. Louise took her sniffling daughter back to bed.

Barbara wheeled Louise down the hall, the two chatting and giggling like old friends. Helen Mae slogged along behind, regaining her composure after signing the release form.

In the hospital room the balance of power shifted. Helen Mae unpacked Louise's brocade bag. "A new night gown," she said. "Nice. But, Mother, tangerine?" Her mother slipped out of her clothes and into the nightgown. The tiny sagging breasts stunned Helen Mae. She hadn't seen her mother naked since their mountain stream skinny dipping adventure with baby Thena, thirty years ago. Helen Mae tucked into the cabinet her mother's lace bra, black underpants, the brown slacks and lime blouse. Her mother was a bundle of contradictions, a thirty-year-old spirit and a sixty-year-old hundred pound body squeezed together into one strong frail woman. After all these years, she didn't know what to make of her.

In the hospital bed Louise pulled up the sheet, white, against tangerine. "Thanks, Honey," she said. "I'm all set now." Jealous of her time alone, Louise couldn't wait to sip the luxury of reading without guilt.

Helen Mae plopped into the visitor's chair. "Jack and I will replace your kitchen window over the sink," she said. "No curtains needed, Mother. (Louise loved sun flowery curtains. Her own mother's curtains were white with ruffles). Did I tell you we'll paint, too? Is flesh pink O.K. for the walls?" From her bag Helen Mae pulled out a swatch of paint and handed it to her mother. She suspected her mother might not like the color, but needed for her to say it. Helen Mae had always loved pink.

Louise remained silent. She tipped her head and pretended to consider the color, then without a word she handed the swatch back to Helen Mae. She didn't feel the need for a new window and she didn't like pink, any pink, especially in the kitchen. Here in this hospital room, with stark white walls and a beige plastic chair, she felt unable to say so, as if the house were no longer hers.

Later that day in Louise's kitchen, Helen Mae and Jack leaned on the Home Depot packing crate, the new window between them, the pink paint and brushes off to the side.

Jack said, "It's her house, Helen Mae. Hers." Jack was ten years older than Helen Mae, who sometimes seemed like a wayward child. He saw Louise as wise and appealing, a quirky friend.

"Someday soon this house will be mine," Helen Mae said. "Why do you side with my mother?" (Leaning into each other Louise and Jack often talked, about what?) "Mother will get used to the window without curtains. Ralph sprouting from his ashes in the herb garden will be clearly visible. Mother's getting older, Jack, and I don't want to have to renovate the kitchen when she dies." Louise had neglected to tell the family of her plan to live to be a hundred.

"Are we redecorating the kitchen for your mother or for you?" Jack asked, surprised that he and his wife of only three years were having this conversation. He was always so careful to avoid conflict with Helen Mae.

Helen Mae stood on the other side of the crate, holding on. "Jack, I'll own this house."

"Yes, but for now it's hers," he said.

Jack moved to the window overlooking the herb garden. He raised the window and put a stick under it. The cool April air freshened the room.

Helen Mae walked out the back door mumbling to herself. "We've got the window. We'll put in the window. We've got the paint. But we're not going to paint. Does mother really care what color the kitchen is?" She stopped, as the red-winged blackbird flashed a wing, landed on the forsythia and fluted. At the herb garden fish's tail, though a month had passed, the soil still appeared freshly turned near the valerian where Ralph's ashes were buried. Bright red tulips celebrated the spot.

Helen Mae paused.

She saw the golden forsythia, the red-winged blackbird, the bright red tulips, and in that moment she knew her mother. "Why would I think she didn't care?" She asked out loud. We'll paint the kitchen green.

In her room at the hospital, a week after the hip replacement surgery and physical therapy, Louise waited for Helen Mae and Jack. On the bed sat her brightly colored brocade bag, its contents spread over the white coverlet. Louise made "keep" and "throwaway" piles. In the keep pile were two bridge tokens, shells from her last walk with Ralph on a beach at the Outer Banks, a smooth stone from a trip to Block Island early last summer, and a couple of dried figs in a plastic bag In the toss pile, receipts from the toaster she recently bought at WalMart, a flair pen that did not work, a pink Kewpie doll on a key chain with an emergency whistle. To Helen Mae's horror, Louise had donated a dollar to a street person in Boston and the woman had given her the doll and the whistle. She struggled to separate the two, but she could not. She wanted to keep the whistle.

Sorting triggered deeper vibrations. Louise considered sound and color. She'd be going home to a newly refurbished kitchen — a pink one. What is the sound of pink? She wondered. Certainly it is not a whistle, a flute, or a snare drum. Even though pink seems light and airy, she thought, it will be a bass guitar, thumping like a heart beat under the song. All the musicians in the world might disagree, but it doesn't matter. Flutes and trumpets get all the attention, she thought, but the bass keeps the whole thing from flying apart. She smiled as she mock played a pink bass guitar. I can live with pink, she thought. I'll bring in trumpeting colors in towels and rugs. There will be no fluting curtains, but tablecloths and wall hangings can carry a melody.

She called Thena on the phone and told her about sorting on the hospital bed. "Mom, it sounds as though you're ready for street hawking — or street walking." They laughed together. "I talked with Helen Mae on the phone yesterday," Thena said. "She said the new window looks beautiful and the kitchen is painted. You'll be surprised, though." Thena chuckled. "That's all I can say."

Thena was like that. One or two sentences or a movement of her body and the essential world moved into sharper focus for Louise. Still holding the phone in one hand and in one grand gesture with the other, Louise swept all the keeps and throwaways — except for the pink doll and the whistle — into the wastebasket. "I've just made the walking choice," she said as Helen Mae walked into the room. "Talk to you later, The."

Despite her less-than-perfect gait, Louise felt ready to return to the *island*. She dressed in her brown slacks and her lime shirt. A little bit of springtime existed for her in the green.

"Good morning, Mother. Don't you look good! Jack's waiting out in the car," said Helen. She picked up her mother's brocade bag and noticed how light it was. "What did you do, Mother, throw away the remnants of your life?

"If I'm going to walk, I'll walk lightly," Louise said. She didn't mention her keep and throwaway piles, jumbled together in the wastebasket. "I've decided to carry nothing unnecessary." She touched the pink Kewpie doll and whistle in her pocket.

Barbara, the nurse's aide, the plump young mother of two whom Louise had befriended from day one, appeared at Louise's bedside. As she assisted Louise from the bedside chair into the transport wheelchair, she asked, "How are you feeling? Are you ready to go home?"

"You know, Barbara," Louise said, straightening her slacks from under her legs and looking directly at Helen, "I actually feel pink."

Helen felt a jolt. She fought back tears. Of what? Regret? Love? Sudden insight into the depth of her mother's love? A flood of emotion swept away her armor. There in the hospital room under bright lights, with Barbara waiting to transport her mother, Helen Mae bent on one knee and said, "Close your eyes, Mother." With her own eyes closed she touched her mother's face, traced around her eyes, her cheekbones, the line of her jaw. Louise absorbed Helen Mae's message without words.

"O.K., open," Helen Mae said, twisting her long hair behind her head into a quick knot as she stood up. "Mother, we have a surprise for you. Jack, The, and I talked about the kitchen — and about you. The new window is in place, but the walls are not pink."

Louise lowered her head and smiled. So that's why Thena chuckled when she said, "...and the kitchen is painted. You'll be surprised...."

Helen Mae nodded to Barbara, who came around behind the wheelchair. Louise reached back and pressed the pink Kewpie doll and the whistle into Barbara's hand. Barbara leaned forward to hear Louise. "For the children," Louise said. "If they don't want the little toys, please bury them somewhere.

—island —

Nearly every writing in this collection is set on
Harmony Island. As I have mentioned before, Harmony is
a fictional name for a real island. The same island name is
used for all writings in this collection: poetry, fiction, and
nonfiction. Hurricane Gloria really did come roaring up
the bay in 1987. This poem arose from the experience of
that hurricane.

Hurricane Gloria vs. Harmony Island

The night before, Harmony paced,
Gathering island strength.
She hauled in and tied down
Then dwelled with memories
Of '38 and '54: the woman
Floating just beyond reach on a rooftop,
Her arms outstretched for a lifeline,
Never to be seen again;
Roads cut off as water washed them under.
Dockside stores swept away

Gloria galloped north.
By daybreak she breathed down Harmony's neck.
Suddenly some felt stranded.
Will there be a ferry?
A broken boat trailer nearly ditched
Its load down the hill
As wind and water rose to taunt.
Remembering those other storms,
Marcy stripped her dockside store.

The unit for fire and rescue counted
Its chainsaws to fight the battle,
Its bandages in case of defeat.
The ferry clutched up and hauled away
The last of those to leave
Before *the storm struck.*
Neighbors swept to aid those
Already down on one knee,
Repairing broken boat trailers,
Making last minute mail deliveries,
Giving rides to those forced to
Move from here to there.

And Gloria marched onward;
Her seas rose above the land
And poised there, holding power,
Threatening inundation.
She cut the Neck in two.
She screamed and hollered,
Pounded docks and pruned the trees.
She hurled her salt to the midland vineyards
And turned our world to brown.

Marcy stood at the store,
As Harmony stood, toe to toe with Gloria.
And the invader stopped at our doorsteps,
Licked at the corner of the dockside store,
And drew back, exhausted.

— the storm struck —

Ah, we remember the storms in vivid detail. Hurricane Jeanne occurred in 2004. Today, after almost thirty years of living on the island, we revel in the stories we share with friends and neighbors. Like everyone else, we continue to live our lives and meet the challenges that each day brings.

Hurricane Jeanne

On a Wednesday morning in October the wind raged and rain slammed against the northeast facing bedroom window. I opened the curtain and saw Matt's dory with the new 40-horsepower engine, looking like a rider on a bucking bronco. I swallowed hard, knowing that Matt would have to go out to save his boat. The dinghy on the pulley line, the one used to row out to the dory, had already sunk.

Downstairs Matt stood, arms crossed, watching the waves. I left him there as I moved sleepily into the bathroom. I preferred not to think.

Jeanne was the tenth hurricane of the season, but Ivan had been the one to worry about. I had tracked each storm from the point of origin to the point of landfall. Once, we had pulled the boats — the dinghy, the dory, and the Sea Hawk — when the track of a hurricane was uncertain. How had this one slid into place without our noticing?

The day before, on Tuesday, a group of community members — Matt and I, Bob Marshall, Eliza Bearse, Rick and Becky Cornell — had made relish at Liza's. It was an all-day affair and nobody had talked about the weather. None of them had boats in the water. By the time we got home and had dinner, we made the mistake of not turning on the weather radio to check out the latest storm.

From hard experience we have learned, when we have a boat moored in front of the house, to keep track of the weather, particularly in the fall, when weather systems are changing. One day the wind blows from the south and the next three from the north. We understand that weather pattern from the days when we first moved to the island in 1980 and we tried to moor our commuting boat in front of the house. Some days we could hardly get a dinghy off the beach. Matt sat in the dinghy, oars poised to row. I stood at the stern of the dinghy in my boots, never high enough to keep the water out, ready to push him off and to jump in so he could then row against the slapping waves.

One infamous time, that standing-holding-off-ready-to—jump-in routine became unnecessary. As we walked down the stairs to the beach at six in the morning, the boat broke loose from the old mooring, to which we had naively tied. We rushed waist deep into the November water to hold the boat off the rocks.

Another time, our first commuting boat, the Sea Ox, moored out in front of the house, was filling with water and in danger of rolling over. As each wave washed over the bow, the Ox rolled uneasily. Matt and I rowed out to it. Since I am the lightest of the two by a hundred pounds, I got in, discovered that the cover from an oil container had come loose and spread oil over the deck, now floating on the water. I slid around and could hardly stay upright to begin bailing. Once again, we saved the boat.

Those and other experiences taught us to be prepared, but Jeanne had come while we dozed. We had been making relish, calmly, happily, carelessly, and now our dinghy had sunk and Matt's dory was in danger.

"I hope Matt will be all right," I thought, knowing his "risk anything to save the boat" way of being. He simply does what needs to be done.

He continued to stand quietly, looking out at the water.

Then, like a clash of cymbals in a quiet room, it struck me that I was going to have to be out there, too. No one else lives near us and there was no time to call anyone mid island.

It was cold. Wet. I get shivery. It was only seven o'clock. Arggh.

Last year at the end of the season I had bought a wet suit so that I would be warm as Matt and I continue our quest to learn sailing. I had never worn it. What had I done with that wet suit?

Searching the coat closet, then the back raincoat closet, I came up with nothing. I knew I was going to get wet out there and I would be freezing cold. Where was that thing? I looked in the closet upstairs, then in my daily clothes closet in our bedroom. There it was. Ah.

I squeezed into the wet suit, drew in my breath and zipped it up. I felt better already. My body heat would stay at least in the core. Matt had said he was ready to go. I grabbed a fleece jacket, then my raincoat and a fleece hat. My legs were bare, my feet in beach shoes.

"Let's drive the big boat out of the docking area," Matt said. The big boat is our Sea Hawk, a twenty-three foot open boat with an outboard engine, the boat we currently use for commuting from the island to the mainland. The dory is Matt's fifteen-foot boat. It is also the one we use for commuting in the summertime, as it uses less fuel than the Sea Hawk. "We'll bring it up to the dory and I'll jump in." That's the way it usually goes. One of us has a plan and we let that fly to see how it feels.

We drove to the dock, a third of a mile down the road, the dock where we keep our Sea Hawk. Immediately, we knew Matt's plan wouldn't work. The tide was so high that it flooded over the dock. Waves crashed and sent huge spray and the water inside the docking area was like a giant's washing machine.

A neighbor's crosstie line hung six inches above the water. We'd never get under that. Only two of us use the docking area for most of the year. Each of us, the mid island neighbor and we, use a crosstie line that the other one has to deal with when he comes into the docking area. Our neighbor's boat was not in the water.

While Matt untied our crosstie line, I released the other crosstie, so that we could drive out of the turbulent docking area. Matt and I boarded our boat and he swung the Sea Hawk out of the docking area and through the wild waves. We found out later that the wind was blowing a steady forty knots and gusting to forty-five or fifty.

Our new plan emerged. I would take the wheel of the Sea Hawk while Matt jumped into the dory. With Matt in the dory and I in the Sea Hawk, we'd go to the Cove, a mile to the west, where Matt would beach his little boat, safely out of the wind. Then we'd bring our Sea Hawk back into Toledo's iron clad docking area. I was glad to hear "we," because it was clear that one of us wouldn't be able to manage the docking at Toledo's alone.

We approached the dory. Both boats reared up and dropped down in opposite rhythms. Matt leaned over the starboard side, as I tried to sidle the Sea Hawk up to the wildly bucking smaller boat. The challenge was to avoid damage to the boats and injury to Matt as he attempted to board the dory.

He hopped into the small boat and I pulled away as waves crashed over the bow of the Sea Hawk and ran out the bailing holes at the stern. I rode up and over the waves, looking back and waiting for Matt, who struggled to release the dory from its mooring line. The wind was so strong that the line from the mooring to the dory was taut. Precariously balanced at the bow of the small boat, he bobbed up and down, up and down, as he drew the boat to the mooring with one hand and unclipped the line from the dory with the other. Barnum and Bailey could have created a water version of its acrobatic circus acts, based on Matt's performance alone.

The dory had never seen rough waters like this. While we knew it was a sea-worthy fifteen footer, it was untried. Using a long handle connected to the motor, Matt stood in the center of the dory and steered toward me through six-foot waves. At one moment he disappeared behind a wall of water, then, lo, he was there again. My challenge was to keep the Sea Hawk heading into the waves and to keep my eye on Matt behind me. Slowly, slowly up and over the waves, we inched toward the cove, a mile away.

Once in the cove, Matt searched carefully for the right place to beach the dory, a soft place, one with no rocks. I circled around in the cove waiting. Once the dory was safely on shore, Matt walked around to the floating dock, where I would attempt to pick him up. I moved in, trying to time my maneuver to exactly the moment he could hop onto the Sea Hawk. The side of the dock faces the northeast. On the other side of the dock, the lee side, Rossi's boat was tied. The northeast wind pushed me and threatened to slam the Sea Hawk into the dock. Shaking with cold now, I slid close to the dock, steady, ready, even as the wind threatened and played. Matt wasn't quite ready, so I backed away, gunning the engine so that I could avoid slamming into the dock. Water poured over the transom and into the stern of the boat.

I circled around and Matt hopped on. I pulled forward, thinking I could veer away from the rocks ahead and drive into deeper water, but the wind was too strong. "No, back her up." He grabbed the wheel and I did, too.

He was right, we had to back away as I had done the first time.

Now, he was behind the wheel and we headed into Toledo's dock, a three sided enclosed area lined with boat-eating iron siding. Several cars of neighbors drew up to watch as we tried to dock our boat. Matt swung the boat around, I leaned over at the bow trying to grab a piling or our line, but I missed them both. "Try again," I yelled. I knew I'd be able to get it the second time.

And we were in, tying up, and breathing normally again.

Back home I stripped off my drenched wetsuit and hung it on one of our wet clothes hooks in the bathroom. I pulled on sweatpants, warm socks, and a sweatshirt. How great it was to be dry! A job well done, I thought.

Several hours later, the wind still howling, Matt said. "The tide is really low. I was going to wait until tomorrow to pull in the dinghy, — the one that had sunk in the morning, — but I'm afraid it will break up. I'm going out to pull it in."

"O.K." I said, cringing at the thought that he'd be out there, getting wet in the cold again. Did I not know what would come next?

I went about my kitchen duties, cleaning the counter, finishing the dishes, when in the door he came.

"I'm going to need a little help," he said. The dinghy is a heavy monster. "I've got it as close to shore as I can get it. We need two of us bailing, because the waves keeps filling it up."

I took my drenched wetsuit off the hook and pulled the wet thing on. No sense in reacting. No sense in spending emotion. What needs to be done, needs to be done.

Down on the rocky beach, I suggested we try to roll the boat rather than bail. With two of us on one side, the wind howling, we lifted the dinghy and emptied the water, even as the waves crashed around us.

To haul the boat to safety higher on the beach, Matt dragged down a huge pipe to put under the boat so that, working together, we could roll that heavy dinghy. Matt pulled in front, I pushed from behind. The dinghy rolled over the pipe. After the dinghy had rolled the length of the pipe, I dragged the pipe away from the stern, through the sand, to Matt so he could place it under the bow, again. He pulled and I pushed, until we had hauled the dinghy to the foot of the embankment where we tied it to a tree.

Then up the stairs we went, together, silently, happy that we had saved our boats.

What is it that forges a partnership, a friendship, a love? We don't always agree on how to do what we have to do. Sometimes we struggle with differences. We have learned, however, that we really are tossed and shaped by the distant sea. We must work together in order to survive — and thrive — in this beautiful craggy place we have chosen to live.

Acknowledgments

For over ten years various members of several different communities have supported and assisted in the improvement of each piece of writing that appears within the collection which eventually came to be entitled: *Tossed and Shaped by the Distant Sea: To Live and To Love.* I am afraid that in naming individuals who have assisted me, I will forget someone. In advance, I ask forgiveness for that oversight and ask for your understanding.

Most profoundly I thank members of my writing group, Educators Writing for Change (EWC) — Jon Appleby, JoAnne Dowd, Jan Grant, Simon Hole and Peggy Silva. For many years, we have spent a weekend together, three or four times a year. During those retreats we critique each other's writings. We ask hard questions and work lovingly together to make each piece of writing the best it can be. Thank you, my friends.

The community, in which I have lived for thirty years, has indeed shaped me and therefore has shaped my writing. I live in a small place, a winter community of one hundred fifty people, ordinary people, a mix of young and old, rich and poor, of well educated and minimally educated. Here one cannot tell, and it does not matter, who is rich or poor, as we all sit at times on the bench at the store waiting for the ferry. Sometimes huddling against the cold, we engage in conversation at the post office, we search for missing persons when the occasion calls for the search. We love each other and we become annoyed with each other. When someone is ill, our individual likes and dislikes do not matter; we help. We are, in the true sense of the word, a community. I have learned so much here about what it means to be human. I am deeply grateful to be part of it all.

Many of the poems in this collection were written under the instruction of S.E. Carlise, for classes at the Harvard School of Writing. The extraordinary experience of being in that program sparked ideas and taught me how exciting it could be to work within the structure of various poetic forms. Two other courses, The Craft of Fiction and Writing Memoir helped me along the way.

Always searching for opportunities to learn to write, I traveled out to Iowa Writers' Workshop one summer, where I enjoyed other writers and, in class, learned about harsh criticism. One writer walked away from a session and threw her manuscript in the wastebasket. As a teacher coach and mentor myself, I was in the right place to receive such feedback, knowing that some had to do with the quality of my writing but that another part of it was the lack of skill on the part of the facilitator. We met and talked about what it means to provide feedback, what skills are needed, how to encourage, be tough, be helpful. I think it became a mutual learning experience.

One year for ten days I traveled to San Francisco to attend classes run by the co-founders and editors of the on-line *Narrative Magazine*: Tom Jenks and Carol Edgarian. What a learning experience that was! Fifteen writers from around the country met each day under guidance of these two exquisite mentors. As a career teacher of writing and literature myself, I learned entirely new ways to look at story. Thank you, Tom and Carol.

Thank you to Jane Maguire and John Silva for reading the entire manuscript, for commenting and critiquing. The collection had taken years and the sequence of writings happened over time. I needed a few people to read through the entire collection.

At that time, Ann Marshall agreed to edit for me, line by line. She had edited for our EWC collection some years ago. *At the Heart of Teaching: A Guide to Reflective Practice* was published by Columbia Teachers College Press. Our writing group learned that she was both respectful and tough in her attention to detail. Thank you, Ann.

Thank you to my family and extended family, who have lived over the years with my talking about this or that writing, who have read now and then a piece for which I needed feedback. Thank you especially to my daughter's husband Jim Strickland, a writer himself, who provided feedback on a story at the right moment, just when it was most needed.

When the collection was finished, my sister, Lenore D. Collins, Ph.D, a career teacher of technology and a publisher, helped me to format the whole manuscript so that it would be acceptable to a publisher. Oh, how patient she was over many hours on the telephone! Thank you. I am deeply grateful, Lenore, for your expertise and sisterly attention.

Finally, thank you to my husband Matt, my daily partner in our ongoing adventure of living in our community on a small island. Matt is the inspiration for so much of my writing and, just as important, he is my friend and critic.

3191421

Made in the USA